POETRY: LOVE & RELATIONSHIPS

A GCSE revision guide
devised and written by Janet Oliver

The right of Janet Oliver to be identified as Author of this Work has been asserted by her in accordance with the Copyright, Designs and Patents Act 1988

First published 2019

ISBN 978-1-9998402-3-5

© Vega Publishing LTD 2019

All rights reserved. No part of this publication may be reproduced, stored in a retrieval system, or transmitted in any form or by any means, electronic, mechanical, photocopying, recording, or otherwise, without the prior written permission of the Publisher.

Restricted copying in the United Kingdom issued by the Copyright Licensing Agency Ltd, Saffron House, 6-10 Kirby Street, London EC1N 8TS

Vega Publishing LTD, 12 Glebe Avenue, Woodford Green, Essex IG8 9HB United Kingdom

Design by Benedict Nangle

Acknowledgements:

'Letters from Yorkshire' by Maura Dooley, from Sound Barrier:Poems 1982-2002 (Bloodaxe Books, 2002). Reproduced with permission of Bloodaxe Books.
'Walking Away' From The Complete Poems by C Day-Lewis. Published by Sinclair Stevenson. Reprinted by permission of The Random House Group Limited. © 1992
'Eden Rock' by Charles Causley from Collected Poems 1951-2000. Published by Macmillan. Reprinted by permission of David Higham Associates.
'Winter Swans' from Skirrid Hill by Owen Sheers. Published by Seren, 2005. Copyright © Owen Sheers. Reproduced by permission of the author c/o Rogers, Coleridge & White Ltd, 20 Powis Mews, London W11 1JN.
'Mother, any distance' from Book of Matches by Simon Armitage and 'Singh Song!' from Look We Have Coming to Dover! by Daljit Nagra reproduced by kind permission of Faber and Faber Ltd.
'Follower' from Death of a Naturalist by Seamus Heaney reproduced by kind permission of Faber and Faber Ltd.
'Before You Were Mine' from Mean Time by Carol Ann Duffy. Published by Anvil Press Poetry, 1993. Copyright © Carol Ann Duffy. Reproduced by permission of the author clo Rogers, Coleridge & White Ltd., 20 Powis Mews, London W11 1JN.

Contents

	Introduction - how to use this book	4
Section 1	**When We Two Parted** - Lord Byron	6
Section 2	**Porphyria's Lover** - Robert Browning	10
Section 3	**Neutral Tones** - Thomas Hardy	14
Section 4	**Winter Swans** - Owen Sheers	18
Section 5	**The Farmer's Bride** - Charlotte Mew	22
Section 6	**Singh Song!** - Daljit Nagra	26
Section 7	**Love's Philosophy** - Percy Bysshe Shelley	30
Section 8	**Sonnet 29** - Elizabeth Barrett Browning	34
Section 9	**Letters From Yorkshire** - Maura Dooley	38
Section 10	**Walking Away** - Cecil Day-Lewis	42
Section 11	**Eden Rock** - Charles Causley	46
Section 12	**Follower** - Seamus Heaney	50
Section 13	**Mother, any distance** - Simon Armitage	54
Section 14	**Before You Were Mine** - Carol Ann Duffy	58
Section 15	**Climbing My Grandfather** - Andrew Waterhouse	62
	Sample Questions & Answers	66
	Glossary - explanation of terms	82

Introduction
How to use this book

The poems explored in this revision guide deal with a wide range of ideas such as the love between parents and children, long distance relationships and forbidden liaisons. They are fantastic poems by inspirational writers and hopefully you have enjoyed reading and discussing them in class.

This guide is written and laid out to help you with your revision of the poems and to ensure that your examination response is focused and clear. It is designed to show you how to include all of the key elements that the examiner is looking for.

- Language analysis with effective use of quotations
- Analysis of form and structure
- Exploration of themes, feelings and attitudes
- Comparison of the poems
- Exploration of the context of the poems

The book is divided into chapters with a box at the top of each section which gives a strong, clear overview of the main theme or idea of the poem.

The section is then dealt with using 5-8 key quotations which are in bold font.

Literary devices are in bold italics. The analysis of each quotation relates directly to the theme or character.

Each quotation is then explored. Some of the points are fairly straight-forward and some are much more analytical.

5 The Farmer's Bride
Charlotte Mew

This *dramatic monologue* explores a farmer's desire to become close to his new wife, chronicling (telling the story of) the disastrous start to their marriage and ending on a note of desperation and loneliness.

'chose'
- The farmer **'chose'** his bride.
- This active *verb* shows how the farmer has full control of the marriage situation and took his pick of the local women. The wife seems to have no choice in the transaction and is therefore powerless. (see context box)

'we... turned the key upon her, fast'
- The wife is locked up after trying to escape.
- There is a sense of the finality of her capture which is emphasised by the poet's use of the comma. This comma creates a pause which underlines the security of the next word: **'fast'**. This establishes a sense of imprisonment; she is locked up like an animal with her freedom as a human being to move around completely curtailed (restricted).
- The farmer has the right to lock her up. The use of the *pronoun* **'we'** suggests that he had local support from villagers who would have seen it as his right to bring his difficult wife home. However, Mew was writing at the time of the emerging Suffragette movement, so Victorian readers might well have started to question this attitude of oppression and control.

Lightbulb Revision: Poetry - Love & Relationships

Context

- Mew began writing at the end of the 19th century, a time which was seeing huge changes to the way women were viewed by society. Mew's work reflects the nature of the Victorian *patriarchal society* and possibly challenges it.
- The wife confuses her husband with her unconventional (strange) ways; Charlotte Mew was also unconventional (she wore trousers and cut her hair short). This lack of understanding that she experienced from society is reflected in her presentation of the farmer's wife, who is also misunderstood.

Form/Structure

- The form of a *dramatic monologue* allows us to experience the speaker's emotions and attitudes. We empathise with him as we are given an insight into rural 19th century attitudes to women and marriage.
- The speaker is male and so the woman is silenced and the reader is only allowed a picture of her through the man's view of her. Yet glimpses of her come through and the portrayal of her is sympathetic.

Comparison

- **Unhappy relationship:** Winter Swans/Neutral Tones
- **Nature:** Sonnet 29/Love's Philosophy
- **Marriage:** Singh Song
- **Control and power:** Porphyria's Lover

💡 **Grade 9 Exploration:** Look at the poem in a different way

Do we sympathise with the farmer or the wife?

- **The farmer:** the poem is from his point of view and he is being kind and respectful, allowing her to sleep upstairs when he could legally force her to sleep with him.
- **The wife:** he is seeing her in terms of her body, objectifying her at the end as he thinks of her **'eyes'** and **'hair'**. He seems to see his wife only in terms of his unsatisfied lust, and this repels us and makes us pity the wife.
- **Both:** This poem shows the pain of an unfulfilled relationship where the couple are not communicating with each other. It is also perhaps a criticism of a system where women are negotiated into marriage and are treated as objects.

The last page of each chapter is the colourful mindmap. It condenses four main points from the chapter into four strands. The information is in a shortened format; if you want to keep your revision really focused, use the mind map to make sure you remember the key features of the chapter.

Marriage: Question & Answer

Compare how marriage is presented in 'Singh Song!' and 'The Farmer's Bride'.

☑ Start with the point that the marriages presented in the two poems are very different

In 'Singh Song', the speaker's marriage is presented as a lively, positive relationship as he enjoys the physical aspect to marriage, describing how they **'made luv/ like vee rowing through Putney'**. The light, tripping *rhythm* and *internal rhyme* of **'vee'/'Putney'** adds to the sense of the poem being a song, perhaps a love song to his unconventional bride. It gives the poem a jaunty tone, showing the speaker's delight in his wife while the humorous *simile* which shows teamwork and physical harmony tells us that they take great pleasure in their sex life. This contradicts the stereotype of the loveless arranged marriage sometimes associated with Indian marriages. However, the marriage in 'The Farmer's Bride' is a relationship where there is no such physical closeness. The end *stanza* highlights the isolation between the farmer and his wife as he says that his wife **'sleeps up in the attic there / Alone, poor maid'**. The *enjambment* emphasises their physical separation, and their loneliness is emphasised with the *caesura* after **'alone'**. We sympathise with the farmer here; he is respecting her desire to not share his marriage bed and the *epithet* **'poor maid'** reveals his feelings of kindness and bewilderment to his unusual wife. We feel pity for her as well as she is so terrified of the marriage bed and so isolated. The companionship of the couple in 'Singh Song', who enthusiastically work together at the sexual side to their relationship, is completely absent in the farmer's marriage.

☑ Move to the point that the marriages are presented in very different settings

The couple in 'Singh Song!' live out their marriage in a town or city and Nagra uses details such as **'concrete-cool'** to show the rather grim urban environment. The hard sounds of the 'c' show the dull, functional environment of the city or town and this contrasts with the soft *alliteration* of the **'silver stool'** where the speaker finds romance and contentment with his wife. It is significant that, despite the mundane, dreary surroundings, the couple can still find romance and magic, encapsulated by the positive *adjective* **'silver'**. Interestingly, the setting for the marriage in 'The Farmer's Bride is the opposite, as the couple live in a rural community surrounded by nature, yet this does not impact positively on their marriage. The farmer uses natural *imagery* to describe his wife who is **'sweet as the first wild violets, she, To her wild self'**. The beautiful *simile* suggests the farmer's admiration for his wife as he uses the image of a flower as a reference from his daily life that he is familiar with. Yet while this *simile* links the wife to nature, it also likens her to the wild and not to 'normal' society. The wife is seen as outside conventional society, challenging the norms of Victorian womanhood as she does not give

---

There is a context section for each poem which explores the social, historical and literary influences of the time that the poet was writing in and how these are reflected in the poem.

Each poem has a separate section which looks closely at structure and form. The comparison section gives suggestions for pairing the poems based on themes.

'Grade 9 Exploration' in each chapter looks at an alternative interpretation of the poem.

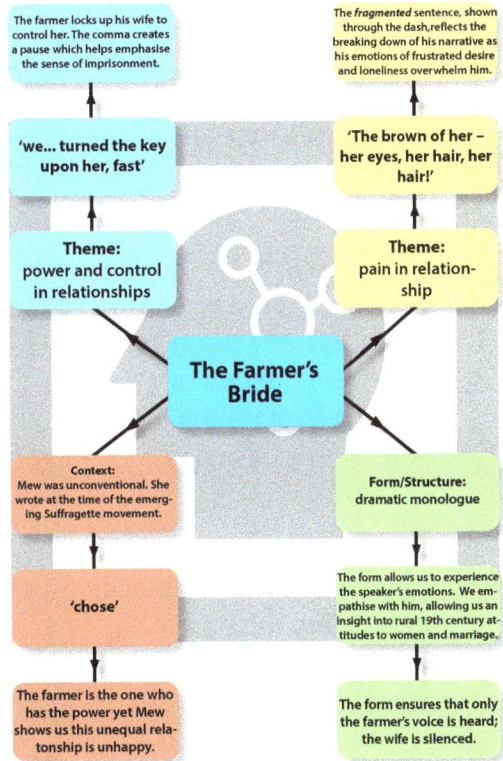

There are eight sample essays. These are based on a four paragraph formula which answers the questions clearly and analytically. If you are wondering what a top level answer looks like, do read it carefully.

1 When We Two Parted
Lord Byron

In this autobiographical poem, Byron catalogues the dissolution (breakdown) of a relationship between the speaker and his lover, revealing the pain and disillusionment that comes with parting.

'In silence and tears'

- Byron uses this phrase, which encapsulates his grief, at the start and at the end of the poem. This shows how the anguish of the speaker will not diminish; the pain of this lost relationship will continue and there is no escape from it.

'knell in mine ear'

- The gossipy news of his lost love's new affair sounds like a bell in the speaker's ear.

- The bell **contrasts** with the earlier theme of silence; Byron is using sound, and the lack of sound, to explore the dissolution of his relationship.

- The **metaphor** of **'knell'** suggests a funeral bell, **symbolising** the death of the relationship. The **monosyllabic** phrase emphasises the leaden despair of the speaker.

6 When We Two Parted   Lightbulb Revision: Poetry - Love & Relationships

'Pale grew thy cheek and cold/Colder thy kiss'

- Combined with the **'chill'** in stanza 2, Byron uses a **semantic field** that creates a lack of warmth, reflecting the bleak nature of his suffering.

- It also shows the **metaphorical** cooling of the relationship as the woman emotionally withdraws from the relationship and the passions of their love fade.

- The word **'cold'** is **repeated** to highlight the shock and grief of the speaker. The **enjambment** also ensures that the second **'Colder'** at the start of the line hits with extra force.

- Bryon uses **accentual verse** to reflect his pain here: the first 4 lines of the **stanza** are written with precise regularity of 5 syllables and 2 stressed syllables. Here, the pattern suddenly changes to a 6 syllable line with 3 stressed syllables which breaks the pattern and startles the reader. This sudden change in the **rhythm** reflects the speaker's trauma, almost as if he is stumbling over his words and breaking down with incoherent grief.

'Thy vows are all broken'

- There is anger at the lack of fidelity and the destruction of trust.

- The **tone** is accusatory; he pins the blame on his lover with a **declarative statement** of how she has broken her promises.

- Byron uses the language of marriage to show how special their love was, yet this also highlights how deeply she has betrayed him.

- This is a very personal poem in that the speaker directly addresses his lover **'thy'** throughout, creating an intimate feel, as if we are eavesdropping on a very personal conversation. The lack of names suggests that Byron was writing about his own experience and hiding his lover's name was a way of protecting her.

- Yet the lack of names also gives this poem a universal appeal. Any reader who has lost a lover can relate to the enduring pain and complexities of emotions.

'shame' 'rue'

- Byron covers a range of emotions to show the complexity of relationships.
- He feels anger and pain but also embarrassment and regret.

Context

- Byron was having a secret affair and wrote this poem about his lover, Lady Webster, who left him for the Duke of Wellington.
- The sense of silence reflects the rigid social mores (conventions) of the time and the need to keep the affair secret.

Form/Structure

- The use of tenses help structure this poem; the 4 *stanzas* move from *past tense*, to *present tense*, to *future conditional tense* at the end with '**if I should meet thee**'. This suggests the extended pain that this relationship has brought and the *future conditional tense* suggests that the negative emotions will not diminish with time and that the pain will endure.
- The regular structure could reflect how the poet is attempting to control his enormous grief by rigid, unchanging *stanzas*.

Comparison

- **End of a relationship:** Neutral Tones/Porphyria's Lover/Winter Swans
- **Pain in a relationship:** Neutral Tones/Winter Swans/Porphyria's Lover
- **Strong Feelings :** Any of the poems

Grade 9 Exploration: Look at the *motif* in a different way

What does the *motif* of silence which threads its way through the poem suggest?

- The *motif* of silence could signify that the lovers have nothing left to say to each other. Communication between them has broken down as feelings have changed.
- Alternatively, the silence could suggest that the poet is almost speechless with grief.
- Another way that the silence is used is to emphasise that the love is clandestine (forbidden) and so must be shrouded in secrecy.

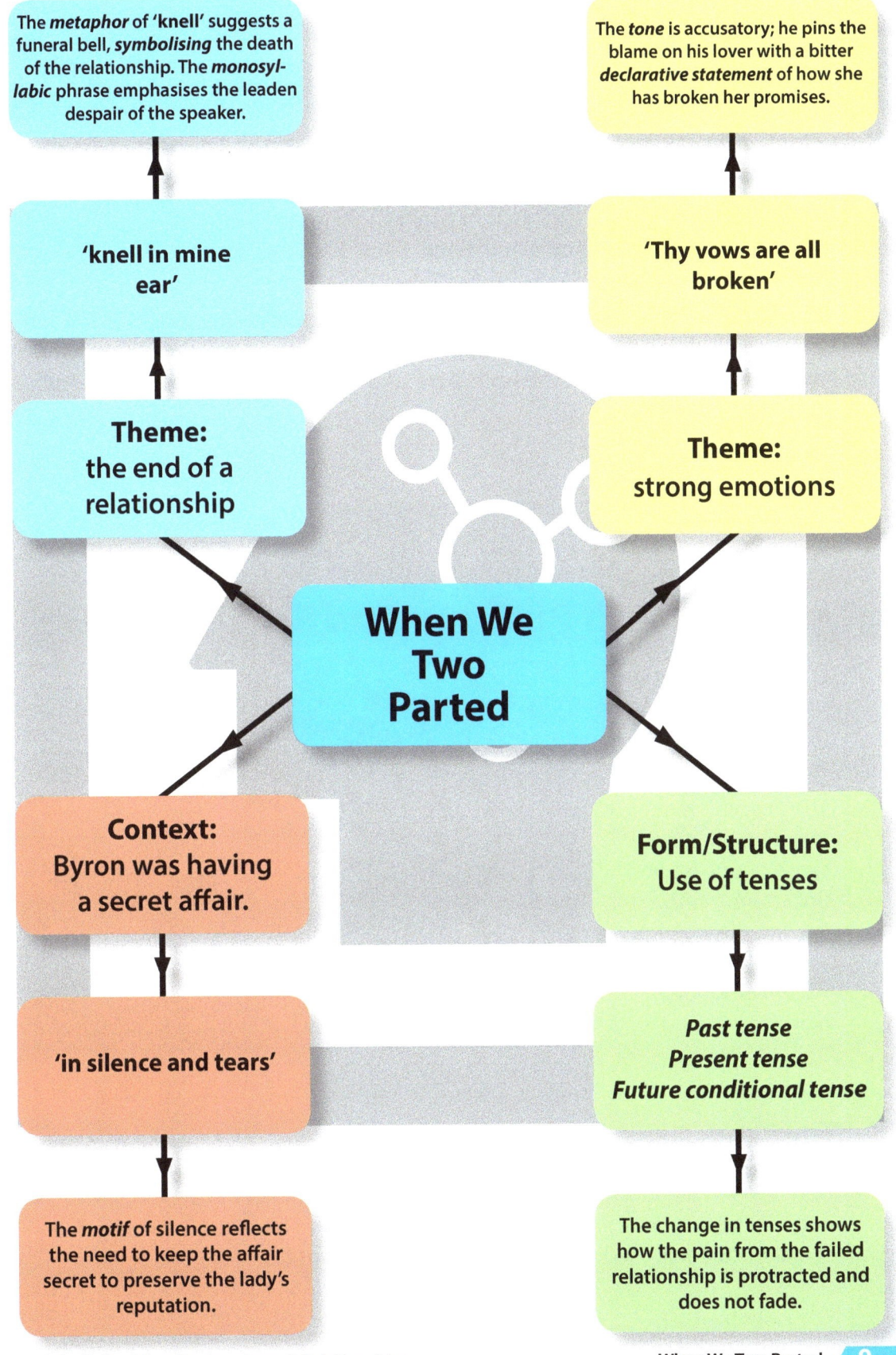

2 Porphyria's Lover
Robert Browning

Browning's *dramatic monologue* tells the story of a disturbed narrator who murders his lover, showing the extremes that love can send us to.

'It tore the elm-tops down for spite'

- The opening of the poem is dense with **pathetic fallacy**. Browning is establishing a bleak, ominous atmosphere through the **personification** of the wind which is seen as vicious in the **verb 'tore'** and malicious with the **noun 'spite'**.

'heart fit to break'

- The destructive weather reflects the narrator's mood. The **metaphor** reveals that the narrator's emotions are being pulled apart, just as the wind is pulling apart the landscape.

- The opening is effective, creating a sense of unease and uncertainty with the volatile weather and the promise of violent emotional pain.

'glided in'

- The **verb** suggests Porphyria's grace and elegance. It reinforces the suggestions within the poem that she is from a different social class to the narrator and that he murders him to prevent her from leaving him for her own level of society. Murder is used as the ultimate form of control.

10 | Porphyria's Lover | Lightbulb Revision: Poetry - Love & Relationships

'That moment she was mine, mine'

- The **repetition** here of the **possessive pronoun** **'mine'** shows the narrator's need to own her and to control her. The sense of drama here increases as the narrator begins to show us his psychopathic tendencies.

'three times her little throat around/And strangled her'

- The precise detail of **'three times'** presents a calm, calculating murderer who is making deliberate choices.

- The **adjective** **'little'** shows Porphyria's vulnerability, directing the reader's response of horror and pity for her.

- The **enjambment** horribly captures the movement of the hair being wrapped around her neck.

- The simple **statement** **'And strangled her'**, which comes at the start of the line, jolts and shocks the reader. There is no tone of the confessional here, no tone of guilt; the narrator is simply stating facts, much as he might say 'and walked home'.

'as a shut bud that holds a bee'

- Far from feeling guilt, the narrator sees this murder as a completely rational action.

- The **simile** here comparing her dead eyelids to a flower bud highlights this idea: that the narrator sees his actions as natural.

'And all night long we have not stirred/And yet God has not said a word!'

- The poem ends in the **present tense**, giving us a sense of timelessness, that the man and his dead lover are still there, unmoving, leaning against each other.

- The last line suggests a complacency: the narrator has not been punished by God so he sees this murder as acceptable.

Context

- The conventions of the Gothic genre, popular with Victorian writers, are clearly used in this poem by Browning; he presents us with a wild, almost supernatural landscape where logical behaviour is being overwhelmed by natural and supernatural influences. In such a world, murderous acts seem normal.

- Victorian society's view of women and their sexuality was much more controlled and restrictive than ours; women were not meant to experience sexual desire, especially outside marriage. Browning could be supporting this view by showing how illicit (immoral) sexual desire needs to be punished. Alternatively, Browning could be challenging this view by showing Porphyria as a victim (see Grade 9 Exploration Box).

Form/Structure

- The **dramatic monologue** allows us insight into the mind of a murderer.
- A completely regular **rhyme scheme** runs through the poem, suggesting a persona who is absolutely in control. Despite the brutal murder, the **rhyme scheme** never alters which suggests a calm, callous lack of feeling on the part of the narrator.
- Alternatively, the regular, rigid **rhyme scheme** could suggest that his mind is deranged and that, to him, the murder is simply a normal, regular event.

Comparison

- **End of a relationship:** Neutral Tones/When We Two Parted/Winter Swans
- **Pain in a relationship:** Neutral Tones/Winter Swans/When We Two Parted
- **Control:** The Farmer's Bride/Love's Philosophy

Grade 9 Exploration: Look at the poem in a different way

What does Porphyria's yellow hair represent?

- **'Yellow hair'** is *repeated* throughout poem. It is a bright colour that is used to **symbolise** a cheerful, sunny personality. Porphyria is positively portrayed and therefore Browning is showing the abuse of women through the violent actions of a man.

- An alternative view is that the **'yellow hair'** is a deliberately sensual *image* that shows that her sexuality needs to be punished. Porphyria behaves outside the rules of conventional society by being alone with her lover; Browning is perhaps showing the consequences of sin and suggesting that she deserves to die.

Porphyria's Lover

Theme: pain of love

'It tore the elm-tops down for spite'
'heart fit to break'

The *metaphor* reveals that the narrator's emotions are being pulled apart, just as the wind is pulling apart the landscape.

Theme: power and control

'Three times her little throat around/ And strangled her'

The *enjambment* horribly captures the movement of the hair being wrapped around Porphyria's neck as the speaker uses violence to possess her.

Context: Browning's Porphyria behaves in a way that is taboo in Victorian society.

Her 'yellow hair' is a bright colour suggesting a cheerful personality so the reader is horrified when she is murdered.

Alternatively, the 'yellow hair' could be a sensual *image* that is used to show that her sexuality needs to be punished.

Form/Structure: *dramatic monologue*

The *dramatic monologue* allows us insight into the mind of a murderer.

The regular *rhyme scheme* shows the calm control of the speaker.

Lightbulb Revision: Poetry - Love & Relationships

3 Neutral Tones
Thomas Hardy

Hardy shares with us a memory of the end of a relationship, focusing on the negative emotions that are experienced at this time.

'Neutral Tones'

- The **metaphorical** title suggests neutrality, a lack of opinion or colour. Immediately, we are introduced to an absence of emotion. This is is not a poem that celebrates the warmth and colour of a healthy relationship.

'sun was white'

- The sun is an unnatural white.
- **Pathetic fallacy** is used to establish a cold relationship, bleached of natural warmth and vitality.

'ash' 'grey'

- The use of colour shows a cold, barren landscape.
- The dull colours reflect the speaker's relationship, which has been washed of life or emotion.
- The **'ash'** tree has hints of a fire that has burnt out, leaving nothing but dust. It **symbolises** the burning out of passion as love is traditionally linked to heat but here the fire, and the relationship, is burnt out and is dead.

'deadest thing/Alive enough to have strength to die'

- Hardy describes his partner's smile as the **'deadest thing'** that is just **'alive enough to have strength to die'**.
- The *metaphor* is bleak; smiles are usually expressions of joy but this one is dead.

'like an ominous bird a-wing...'

- The *simile* compares the lover's grin to a prophetic bird of doom.
- It is an omen that forecasts the end of their relationship.
- The *ellipsis* marks a turn in the poem, as the poet finishes his memory. It also suggests that the memory lingers on in the poet's mind.

'God-curst sun'

- Hardy describes the sun as **'God-curst'**.
- Hardy's writing often explored the idea of divine indifference (lack of caring from God). Here we are shown a **'God-curst sun'**, creating an incredibly negative atmosphere.
- We wonder whether the couple are also being punished by God in the failure of their relationship; Hardy's writing consistently explores this sense of punishment, of an unfeeling, cold divine presence which treats humans harshly.

Context

- Hardy's first marriage was an unhappy one; his difficult relationships with women are reflected here in this poem.
- Hardy's writing was often pessimistic and there is a poignant sense of an end of an era with the end of the relationship. This sense of the end of an era could reflect a wider perspective, referencing the rapid industrialisation of Britain which had so many negative consequences for the poor in the rural areas where Hardy lived.

Form

- The poem's first three **stanzas** are written in the **past tense**, capturing the sense of memory.
- The last **stanza** is in the **present tense**, suggesting that the memory is fresh in his mind and that he revisits it. This is also encapsulated (shown) by the **circular structure**; the poem begins and ends with the pond, illustrating how it has influenced his life. Like the still water of the pond does not move, he also has not moved on; the **circular structure** shows that he cannot escape this unhappy memory.

Comparison

- **End of a relationship:** When We Two Parted/Porphyria's Lover
- **Pain in a relationship:** Porphyria's Lover/Winter Swans/When We Two Parted
- **Use of memory:** Before You Were Mine/Eden Rock
- **Strong Feelings :** Any of the poems

Grade 9 Exploration: Look at the poem in a different way

Is the poem really neutral?

- **Yes:** The use of commas in the final stanza creates a disjointed, awkward pace which reflects the speaker's disconnection with the situation. The **anaphora** of **'and' 'and'** with **monosyllabic** words results in a heavy, defeated **tone** at the end. Hardy uses this to end his poem on this dull, lifeless **rhythm** to show his lack of emotion about the relationship.

- **No:** His language choices clearly show bitterness, not neutrality. The statement that **'love deceives'** reflects his bitter disillusionment with love and suggests that he is angry and blames his partner for the break-up.

16 Neutral Tones Lightbulb Revision: Poetry - Love & Relationships

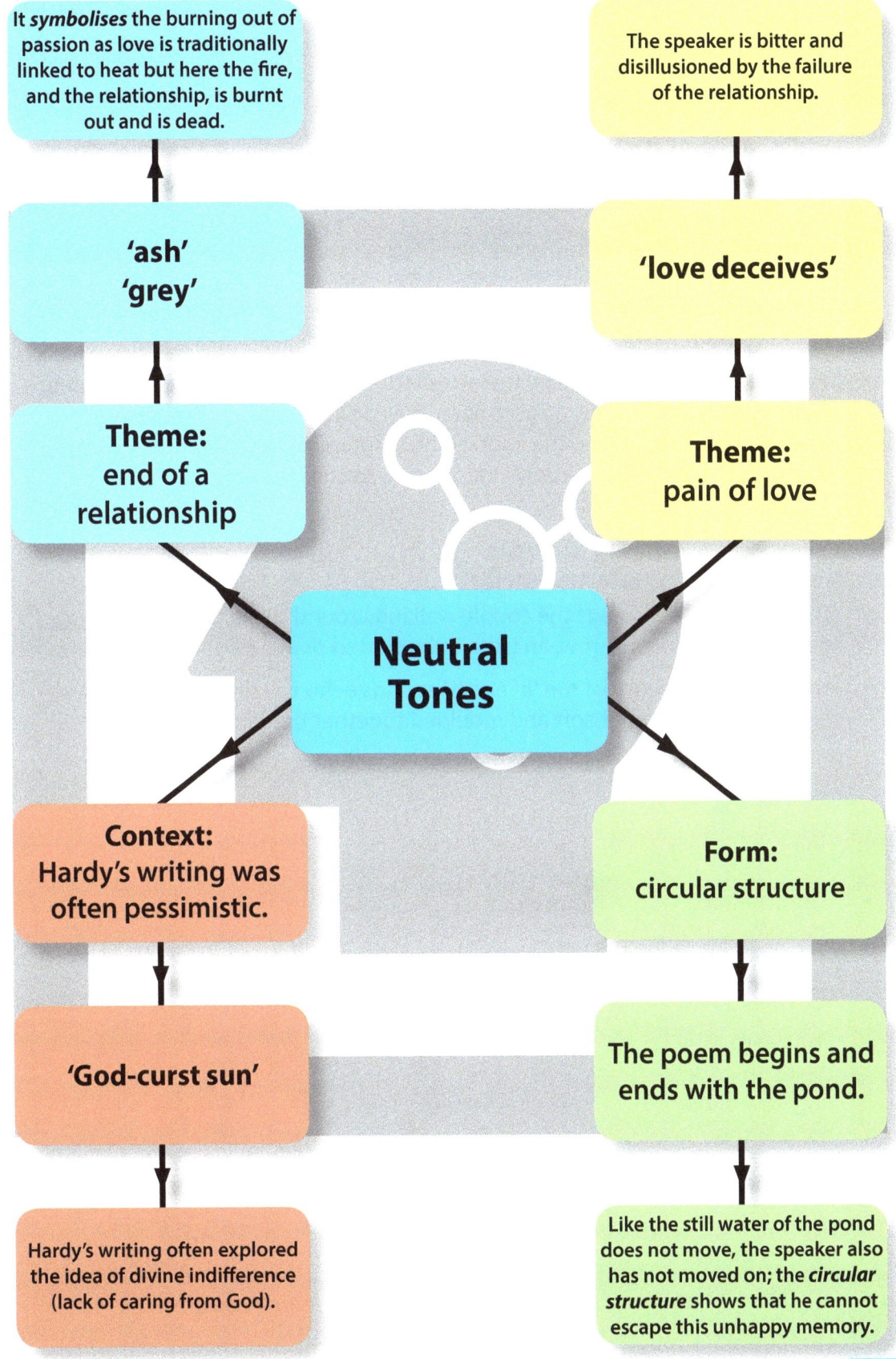

4 Winter Swans
Owen Sheers

Sheers describes an afternoon walk by a lake in winter where a couple who are distanced from each other are reconciled.

'waterlogged earth/gulping for breath'

- The **personification** of the muddy ground struggling to breath is an uncomfortable *image*.
- The **pathetic fallacy** of the post-storm setting and the *image* of a suffocating earth establish an uneasy atmosphere. The natural world is unsettled and struggling and so reflects the couple's disharmonious relationship. It seems that the couple are also struggling to speak, to communicate.

'skirted the lake, silent and apart'

- The **verb 'skirted'** shows the couple walking around the lake but it also suggests there has been a row, an issue to be skirted or avoided.
- The hard **consonance** of the **'k'** and **'t'** sounds echo the rift between the couple; the sounds are not soft and moulded together but jarring and sharp.

'until the swans came'

- **'Until'** marks the **volta** and the mood of the poem changes.
- The swans in their natural setting now bring hope to the arguing couple.

'tipping in unison'

- The birds are a model of harmony and cooperation; **'tipping'** their heads suggests giving in and acceptance.
- This motion of compromise establishes the swans as a **symbol** of unity and cooperation.

'slow-stepping'

- The **verb** shows that the couple now move together in harmony. This is in direct **contrast** to the earlier hostile **verb** of **'skirting'**.
- There is a sense of dynamic (active) movement, that the couple are moving on from their rift, healing their relationship as they progress onwards.
- The **sibilance** here is soft, showing the couple are not hostile anymore but are warming to each other.

'stilling water' 'afternoon light'

- The natural setting now represents hope and calm.
- Sheers uses this as a device to record the change in mood and the shift in the relationship.

'like a pair of wings settling after flight'

- The beautiful **simile** shows the couple's hands joining together.
- The **image** links the couple with the swans who **'mate for life'**. The couple are now like the faithful swans, joining together to stand by each other despite rocky times.
- The word **'pair'** places them together, sealing the sense of unity.

Context

- 'Winter Swans' is part of a collection of poems from an anthology called 'Skirrid Hill' which often explores the idea of separation and divorce.
- The poem explores a universal experience; few relationships are free from any disagreements and arguments.

Form/Structure

- The poem finishes with a two line **stanza**, **symbolising** the pairing of the two lovers. This marks a change from the previous three line **stanzas** and shows at the end the couple have healed their disagreement.
- **'Until the swans came'**: **'until'** marks the **volta** and the mood of the poem changes. The swans in their natural setting now bring hope to the estranged (arguing) couple.

Comparison

- **Arguing couples:** Neutral Tones
- **Nature:** Letters from Yorkshire/Neutral Tones
- **Pain:** When We Two Parted/The Farmer's Bride/Porphyria's Lover

Grade 9 Exploration: Look at the poem in a different way

Does this poem celebrate reunion or are the couple still arguing at the end?

- **Reunited:** The structure suggests that the couple are reconciled (back together) as the final **couplet** reflects the pairing of the couple. The **simile** of the hands being like wings also links the couple to the faithful swans who **'mate for life'**.
- **Still distanced:** There still is a sense that the couple are still not communicating; their hands came together **'somehow'**. The word **'somehow'** could be positive and suggest that their hands instinctively reach for each other. Alternatively, the word **'somehow'** could reflect how their hands meet almost by accident and that it is not a planned action.

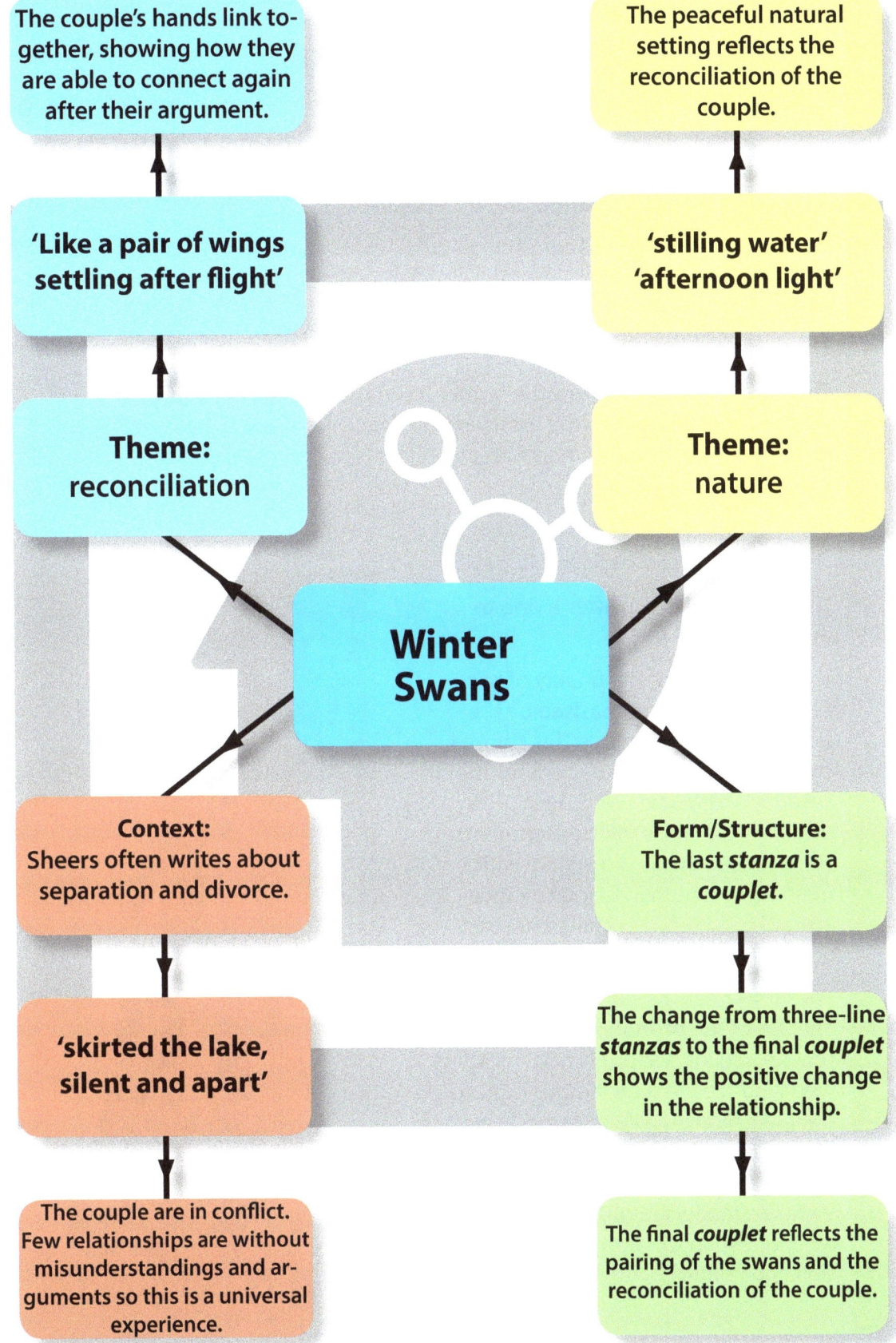

5 The Farmer's Bride
Charlotte Mew

This *dramatic monologue* explores a farmer's desire to become close to his new wife, chronicling (telling the story of) the disastrous start to their marriage and ending on a note of desperation and loneliness.

'chose'

- The farmer **'chose'** his bride.
- This active **verb** shows how the farmer has full control of the marriage situation and took his pick of the local women. The wife seems to have no choice in the transaction and is therefore powerless (see context box).

'we... turned the key upon her, fast'

- The wife is locked up after trying to escape.
- There is a sense of the finality of her capture which is emphasised by the poet's use of the comma. This comma creates a pause which underlines the security of the next word: **'fast'**. This establishes a sense of imprisonment; she is locked up like an animal with her freedom as a human being to move around completely curtailed (restricted).
- The farmer has the right to lock her up. The use of the **pronoun 'we'** suggests that he had local support from villagers who would have seen it as his right to bring his difficult wife home. However, Mew was writing at the time of the emerging Suffragette movement, so Victorian readers might well have started to question this attitude of oppression and control.

'sweet as the first wild violets, she, /To her wild self'

- The **simile** compares the wife to flowers that grow wild, linking her to nature rather than to 'normal' society. She is seen as outside conventional society and so challenges the norms of Victorian womanhood.

- The positive **simile** suggests the farmer's admiration. He uses the **image** of a flower as a reference from his daily life that he is familiar with.

- Yet the **repetition** of **'wild'** is used by the poet to emphasise the farmer's confusion as to how to form a relationship with someone so unconventional, so untamed.

'She sleeps up in the attic there / Alone, poor maid'

- The final **stanza** highlights the isolation between the farmer and his wife as they sleep apart.

- The **enjambment** emphasises the physical separation and the loneliness is emphasised with the **caesura** after **'alone'**.

- We sympathise with the farmer here; he is respecting his wife's desire to not share his marriage bed and the **epithet** **'poor maid'** suggests his feelings of kindness and bewilderment to his unusual wife. We feel pity for her as well, so terrified of the marriage bed and so isolated (see Grade 9 Exploration).

'The brown of her – her eyes, her hair, her hair!'

- This is a painful ending to the poem as the farmer thinks about his wife's hair and eyes. The farmer's lust is evident in the focus of her physical characteristics. The **repetition** here emphasises how his frustrated desire is at the forefront of his mind.

- It is interesting that he mentions **'eyes'** and **'hair'** but not her mouth or lips. This emphasises her silence in this marriage and the lack of communication.

- The **fragmented** line with the **dash** shows the breaking down of his narrative as his emotions overwhelm him.

Context

- Mew began writing at the end of the 19th century, a time which was seeing huge changes to the way women were viewed by society. Mew's work reflects the nature of the Victorian **patriarchal society** and possibly challenges it.
- The wife confuses her husband with her unconventional (strange) ways; Charlotte Mew was also unconventional as she wore trousers and cut her hair short. This lack of understanding that she experienced from society is reflected in her presentation of the farmer's wife, who is also misunderstood.

Form/Structure

- The form of a **dramatic monologue** allows us to experience the speaker's emotions and attitudes. We empathise with him as we are given an insight into rural 19th century attitudes to women and marriage.
- The speaker is male and so the woman is silenced and the reader is only allowed a picture of her through the man's view of her. Yet glimpses of her come through and the portrayal of her is sympathetic.

Comparison

- **Unhappy relationship:** Winter Swans/Neutral Tones
- **Nature:** Sonnet 29/Love's Philosophy
- **Marriage:** Singh Song
- **Control and power:** Porphyria's Lover

Grade 9 Exploration: Look at the poem in a different way

Do we sympathise with the farmer or the wife?

- **The farmer:** the poem is from his point of view and he is being kind and respectful, allowing her to sleep upstairs when he could legally force her to sleep with him.
- **The wife:** he is seeing her in terms of her body, objectifying her at the end as he thinks of her **'eyes'** and **'hair'**. He seems to see his wife only in terms of his unsatisfied lust, and this repels us and makes us pity the wife.
- **Both:** This poem shows the pain of an unfulfilled relationship where the couple are not communicating with each other. It is also perhaps a criticism of a system where women are negotiated into marriage and are treated as objects.

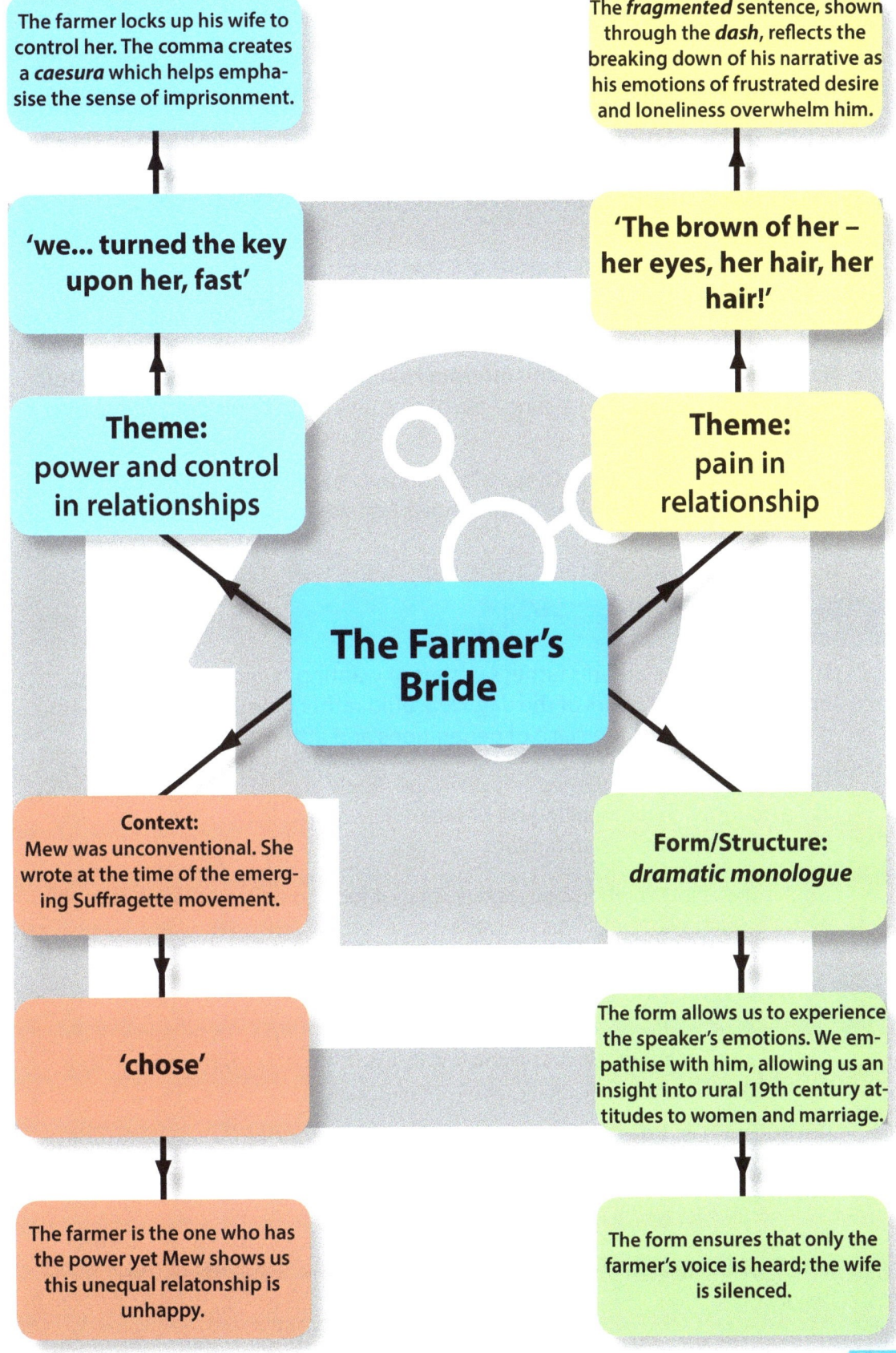

6 Singh Song!
Daljit Nagra

Nagra presents a relationship between a married Punjabi couple, using humour and vivid images to show an unconventional relationship which challenges traditional stereotypes about the lives and characters of immigrants.

'made luv/like vee rowing through Putney'

- The speaker talks enthusiastically about his sex life.
- The light, tripping **rhythm** and **internal rhyme** - **'vee' 'Putney'** - adds to the sense of the poem being a song - perhaps a love song to his unconventional bride.
- It gives the poem a jaunty tone, reflecting the speaker's delight in his wife while the humorous, cheeky **simile** shows he takes great pleasure in their sex life.

'But ven nobody in, I do di lock'

- The speaker is defying his father's wishes of wanting him to keep the shop open and work all hours of the day. He would rather be making love with his new bride, showing the clash of generations and attitudes.
- There is a hint at a repressive culture in the **'lock'** and he is perhaps behaving like a naughty child, sneaking off in secret. This shows the power of the older generation in South Asian families.
- Yet it is the speaker who chooses to turn that lock, to enjoy his wife's company; he is taking control of his daily life.

'Hey Singh, ver yoo bin?'

- The italicised **stanzas** work as a **chorus**; customers demand to know where the speaker has been.
- The question is rude and aggressive and shows the contemptuous attitudes of the local people. It contrasts with the positive marital relationship being described.
- It reminds the reader of the racism and hostility of the community. The **repetition** of the **chorus** emphasises this and shows the regularity of the complaints.

'tiny eyes ov a gun/ and di tummy ov a teddy'

- The speaker gives us contrasting *images* of his wife.
- She is seen as focused and watchful with the **'tiny eyes'** and there is an element of danger with the *metaphor* of a gun. The speaker challenges the stereotype of the compliant Indian wife.
- The next *image* of the **'teddy'** suggests softness and warmth and comfort, showing that relationships can be complex and multi-layered.
- This fits into one of the messages of the poem: that we can't label other people in fixed certain ways.

'concrete-cool' 'silver stool'

- Nagra uses *alliteration* here to show the rather grim urban environment.
- The hard sounds of the **'c'** show the dull, functional environment of the city or town.
- This *contrasts* with the soft *sibilance* of **'silver stool'** where the speaker finds romance and companionship with his wife.
- Despite the mundane surroundings, the couple can still find romance and magic, encapsulated by the positive *adjective* **'silver'**.

'From di stool each night I say/-Is priceless baby'

- The relationship between the speaker and his wife is a strong one; the ending of the poem shows them sitting together looking at the moon, contradicting the stereotype of loveless arranged Indian marriages.
- The *repetition* of these lines **'from di stool'** shows that it's a nightly ritual between them, emphasising their closeness and joy in each other.
- He clearly values his wife - **'priceless'** - above money, perhaps showing a shift in attitude from his parents' and grandparents' attitudes.

Context

- Daljit Nagra was born in London to Sikh Punjabi parents. His poetry reflects his background and he once commented that he is 'obsessed with Asian-ness'.
- The bride's choice of clothing such as a **'tartan sari'** reflects this mixing of two cultures; the desire to hold onto traditional values and the desire to be part of a new culture.
- Many immigrants also experienced racism and the *chorus* of **'Hey Singh, ver you bin?'** illustrates this.

Form/Structure

- The poem takes the form of a **dramatic monologue**, allowing us to see into his life and emotions. The **dialect** creates a strong personal voice, showing us that this is a personal story but also one that can be used to challenge general stereotypes.
- **'Hey Singh, ver yoo bin?'** The italicised **stanzas** work as a **chorus** which **contrasts** with the positive relationship being described. The **repetition** of the **chorus** emphasises this and shows the regularity of the complaints and the continuity of racism.

Comparison

- **Marriage:** The Farmer's Bride
- **Happiness in relationships:** Sonnet 29/Love's Philosophy
- **Parental clashes:** Follower

Grade 9 Exploration: Look at the poem in a different way

Are the couple truly happy?

- **Yes:** **'Made luv /like vee rowing through Putney'** There is a sense of genuine pleasure and union in this **simile** which shows the couple moving in partnership. The cheeky sense of humour creates a cheerful, joyous relationship.

- **No:** The couple is repressed with the reference to the **'lock'** suggesting a restrictive culture. And they both dream of escape, looking longingly every night at the **'brightey moon'** as they are surrounded by urban **'concrete-cool'**. Also, clear anger is shown as the bride is **'effing at my mum'**; this reflects frustration and rebellion. The couple are having to deal with a lot - racism, parental pressure, hard work. This marriage is not one of complete bliss.

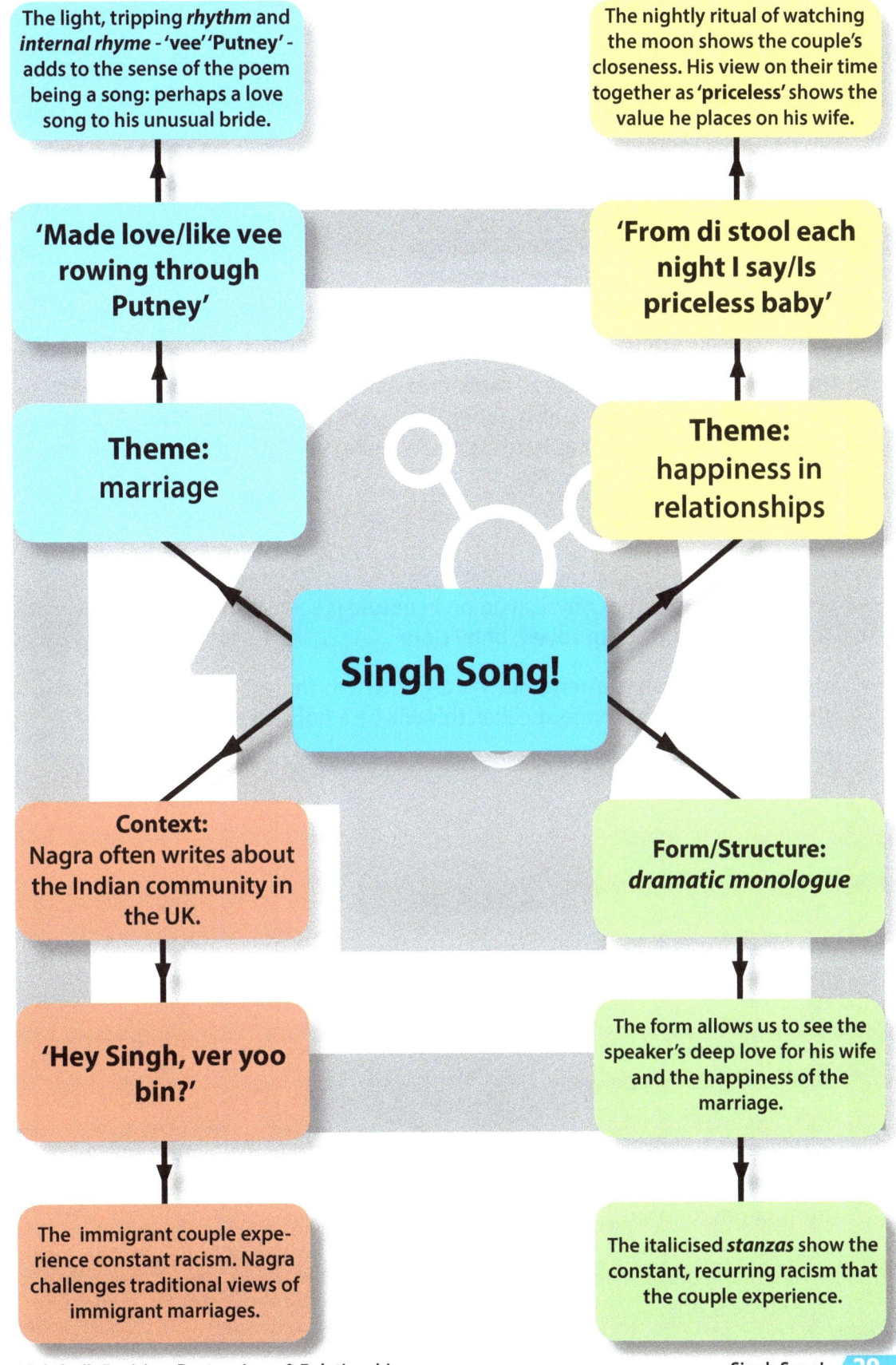

7 Love's Philosophy
Percy Bysshe Shelley

Shelley uses this poem to present a convincing argument to an unknown loved one that they should most definitely be together.

'The fountains mingle with the river'

- The poem opens with a series of facts about the interdependence of nature. Shelley points out that natural elements are all connected with each other.

- He is asserting that because all aspects of nature interconnect, the love between men and women is also a completely natural act. By choosing his evidence and presenting it as hard fact, he is being very convincing and leaves no room for dissent (argument).

'law divine'

- Shelley points out that physical union in nature is seen as **'divine'**. This means that it is sanctioned (approved) of by God.

- He is using religion to strengthen his argument as there is a suggestion that if the lady does embrace the speaker, this will be a holy act and God will approve.

'See the mountains kiss high Heaven'

- Shelley commands the lady to look at the moutains touching the sky.

- The *imperative verb* **'see'** gives her no option but to follow the command.

- The positive *image* of the mountains reaching to the sky works to reinforce the argument (see context box).

Love's Philosophy — Lightbulb Revision: Poetry - Love & Relationships

'disdain'd'

- The second **stanza repeats** the argument, suggesting that if a flower **'disdain'd'** (rejected) another, then this would flout (break) the laws of nature.
- The logical conclusion is that the woman should kiss the speaker otherwise she will be seen as unnatural.

'and the sunlight' 'and the moonbeams'

- Shelley uses a range of natural elements to prove his point.
- Here he uses **images** of light to symbolise hope and joy, emulating the optimism and rapture (intense joy) experienced by the love between two humans.
- It is significant that he mentions light by day and night, suggesting that love is a perpetual (constant) emotion.
- **Anaphora** is used here to give added weight to Shelley's argument. It is used to move the argument towards its conclusion by building up the evidence in a list.

'What are all these kissings worth/ If thou kiss not me?'

- Shelley ends the poem with a **rhetorical question** which is intentionally disarming.
- Shelley is using it to manipulate his potential lover because it almost forces the questioned lady to answer 'Of course I will kiss you!' To reject him would be to reject nature and God and the laws of the universe.
- This last line of the poem works as a neat ending to the culmination (conclusion) of ideas that have been built up throughout the poem.

Context

- Shelley was a Romantic poet and embraced the beauty and power of Nature. Having lived in mountainous Switzerland, he was inspired by the scenery and made reference to this in his poem.

- **'High Heaven'** works with **'divine'** to create a *semantic field* of religious *imagery* that slots in neatly with the theme of nature. The implication here is that the pairing of man and woman is a natural act that is blessed by God. Here, Shelley is using religion to strengthen his argument although he was himself an atheist. This would be especially relevant to most 19th century readers to whom Christianity was a fundamental part of life.

- Shelley was interested in the radical notion of free love and this poem, with its reliance on the naturalness of a physical relationship, reflects this.

- Shelley is continuing the literary tradition of seduction by poetry that was used by poets such as Donne and Marvell.

Form/Structure

- Shelley *structures* his poem as two *octaves* that build up a clever argument, adding layers of logic and persuasive devices to convince his lady that she must consent (agree) to be his lover.

- Each *stanza* ends with a *rhetorical question* that engages the listener and ensures that the argument is seen as convincing.

Comparison

- **Happiness in relationships:** Singh Song!/Sonnet 29
- **Nature:** Letters from Yorkshire
- **Power in a relationship:** The Farmer's Bride/Porphria's Lover

Grade 9 Exploration: Look at the poem in a different way

Is the poem is a pure celebration of the naturalness and joy of love?

- **Yes:** Shelley uses a range of natural elements such as **'sunlight'** and **'moonbeams'** to prove his point. He uses *images* of light to *symbolise* hope and joy, emulating the optimism and rapture (intense joy) experienced by the love between two people.

- **No:** The positive message is completely undercut by the manipulative way that Shelley has constructed his argument. It is *structurally* so cleverly put together that it rings of a cynical attempt at seduction rather than as a genuine outpouring of love. The sense of artifice or falsehood is even more noticeable if we remember that Shelley uses religion to strengthen his point yet he was himself an atheist.

Love's Philosophy

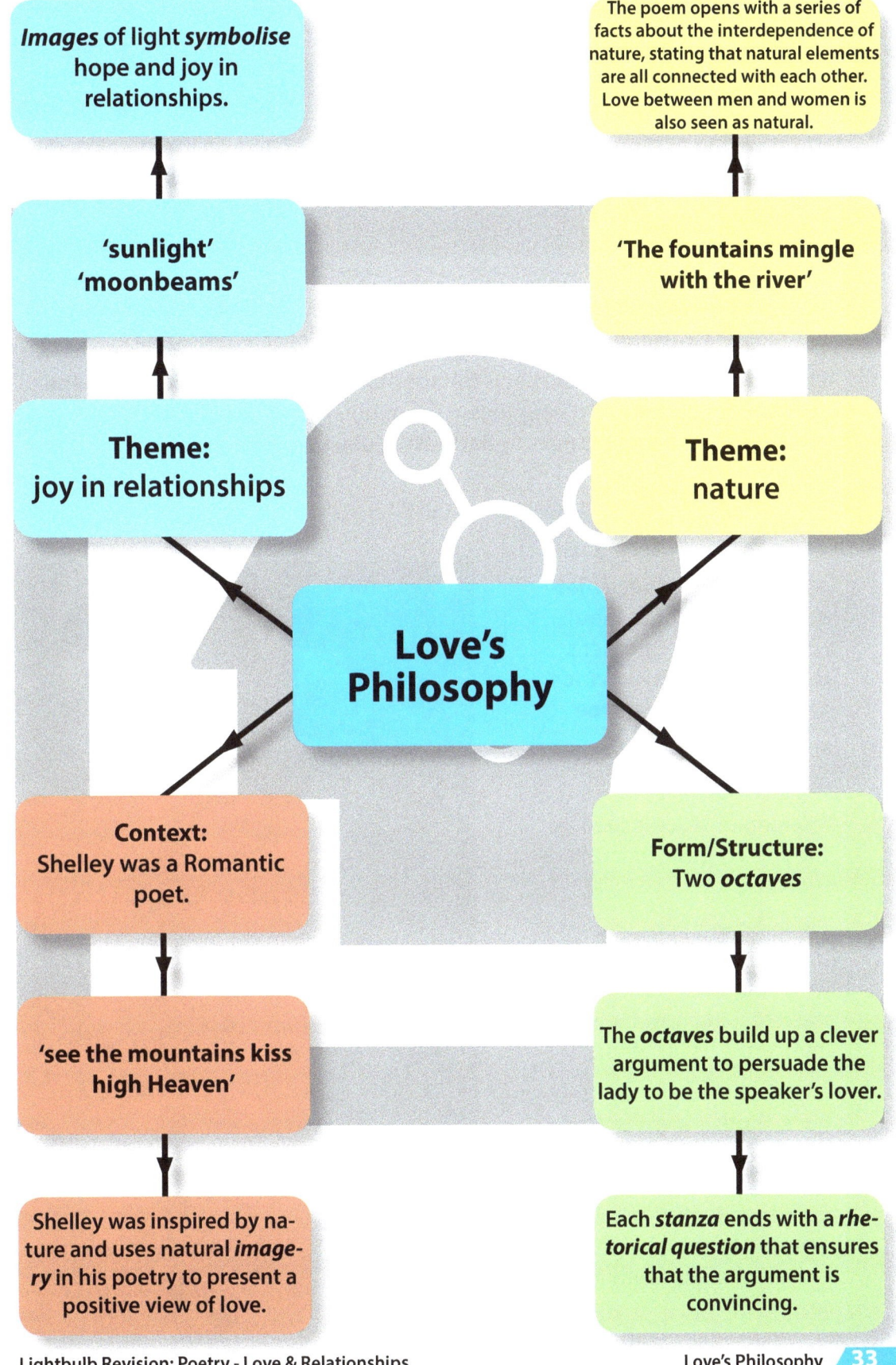

8 Sonnet 29 - 'I think of thee!'
Elizabeth Barrett Browning

Barrett Browning explores the all-consuming nature of love as the speaker declares how she continually thinks of her lover and longs to be with him.

'I think of thee!'

- A positive *exclamatory sentence* opens the *sonnet*. **'I think of thee!'** is a simple, factual *statement* that shows how the absent lover is in her thoughts.

- The *exclamatory sentence* shows the spontaneous calling out, revealing the speaker's excitement and happiness as thoughts of her lover fill her mind. **'Thee'** tells us that she is directly addressing one person.

'twine and bud/About thee'

- A *conceit* or *extended metaphor* is used throughout the poem of the speaker's thoughts being **'wild vines'** and her loved one a **'tree'**.

- Natural *imagery* is used to reflect their love.

- Interdependency is seen as the vines **'twine'** or interlace together.

- *Enjambment* here echoes the movement of the vine wrapping itself around the tree, showing how their love interconnects together.

- There are sexual connotations. **'Bud'** is a *symbol* for female genitalia, **'twine'** suggests the physical sexual union of two bodies with **'wild'** referring to the passionate lack of inhibition within the sexual act.

'O my palm-tree'

- The speaker calls her lover **'my palm-tree'**.
- This *image* is a reference to the Bible; palm trees were used to welcome Jesus into Jerusalem. Barrett Browning was very religious so this choice of *metaphor* shows how divine and sacred her love is.
- **'Palm tree'** could also suggest an oasis in the desert, highlighting how her lover is someone who is saving her from the barrenness and loneliness of single life.
- It could also be a *metaphor* to suggest faith, showing how she believes in their love, and how it is a cornerstone of her life.

'set thy trunk all bare'

- The *extended metaphor* of the tree continues as she suggests that the tree's trunk should be naked.
- There are sexual connotations here with the sense of nakedness. Victorian society would require any sexual references to be subtle so the speaker just hints at the idea of seeing her lover's naked body.

'I do not think of thee - I am too near thee'

- The *sonnet* concludes with the speaker stating that she no longer needs to think of him once they are physically together.
- There is a sense of completeness and fulfilment at the end, highlighting the positive nature of their love.

Context

- Barrett Browning wrote this **sonnet** and others in the 'Sonnets of the Portuguese' to her fiance as an expression of love. The love story of Elizabeth Barrett Browning and Robert Browning was one of genuine passion and life-long dedication, and this is reflected in these **sonnets**.
- She was very religious and so the religious *imagery* of the **'palm tree'** shows this faith.
- Victorian society would require any sexual references to be subtle, hence the ambiguous references to the tree, bud and vines.
- The use of **'thee'** is old-fashioned for the time of writing. However, Barrett Browning was a Romantic poet and Romantic poets often looked back to an idealised past so the use of **'thee'** highlights the idealism of her love.

Form/Structure

- The **sonnet** form used is a traditional form for love poems, and this is a very personal, very passionate love poem.
- A **sonnet** presents an argument and this **sonnet** declares how the lover consumes her thoughts when apart and when he is actually with her, he completes her.
- The *rhyme* of **'tree' 'thee' 'see'** holds the poem together, reflecting how the vines and the tree are also interconnected, just like the love the speaker has for her lover.

Comparison

- **Parted couples:** Letters from Yorkshire
- **Nature:** Letters from Yorkshire/Love's Philosophy
- **Pleasure in a relationship:** Love's Philosophy/Singh Song!

Grade 9 Exploration: Look at the poem in a different way

Is this a healthy, positive relationship?

- **No:** There is an uneasy sense that this is an obsessive love. The speaker states that **'there's nought to see'** as the vines cover the tree so fully that there's nothing left visible. The *image* suggests that the speaker has an all-consuming need to contain and cover the beloved which seems smothering and unhealthy.
- **Yes:** The tree/vine *imagery* is a natural one with the **verb 'bud'** showing how she blossoms through her relationship with him. The **extended metaphor** reveals a nurturing, healthy, growing relationship.

I think of thee!

Theme: joy of relationships

'I think of thee!'

The *exclamatory statement* that opens the poem shows the speaker's happiness and enthusiasm.

Theme: nature

'twine and bud/ About thee'

The vine/tree *imagery* reflects the natural love between the couple.

Context: Barrett Browning was religious.

'palm tree'

The use of the palm tree, with its Biblical associations, shows how her love is based on faith.

Form/Structure: *sonnet*

The *sonnet* form is traditionally used for love poems.

The *rhyme* of 'tree' 'thee' 'see' holds the poem together, reflecting how the vines and the tree are also interconnected, just like the speaker and her lover are linked.

Lightbulb Revision: Poetry - Love & Relationships
Sonnet 29 - 'I think of thee!'

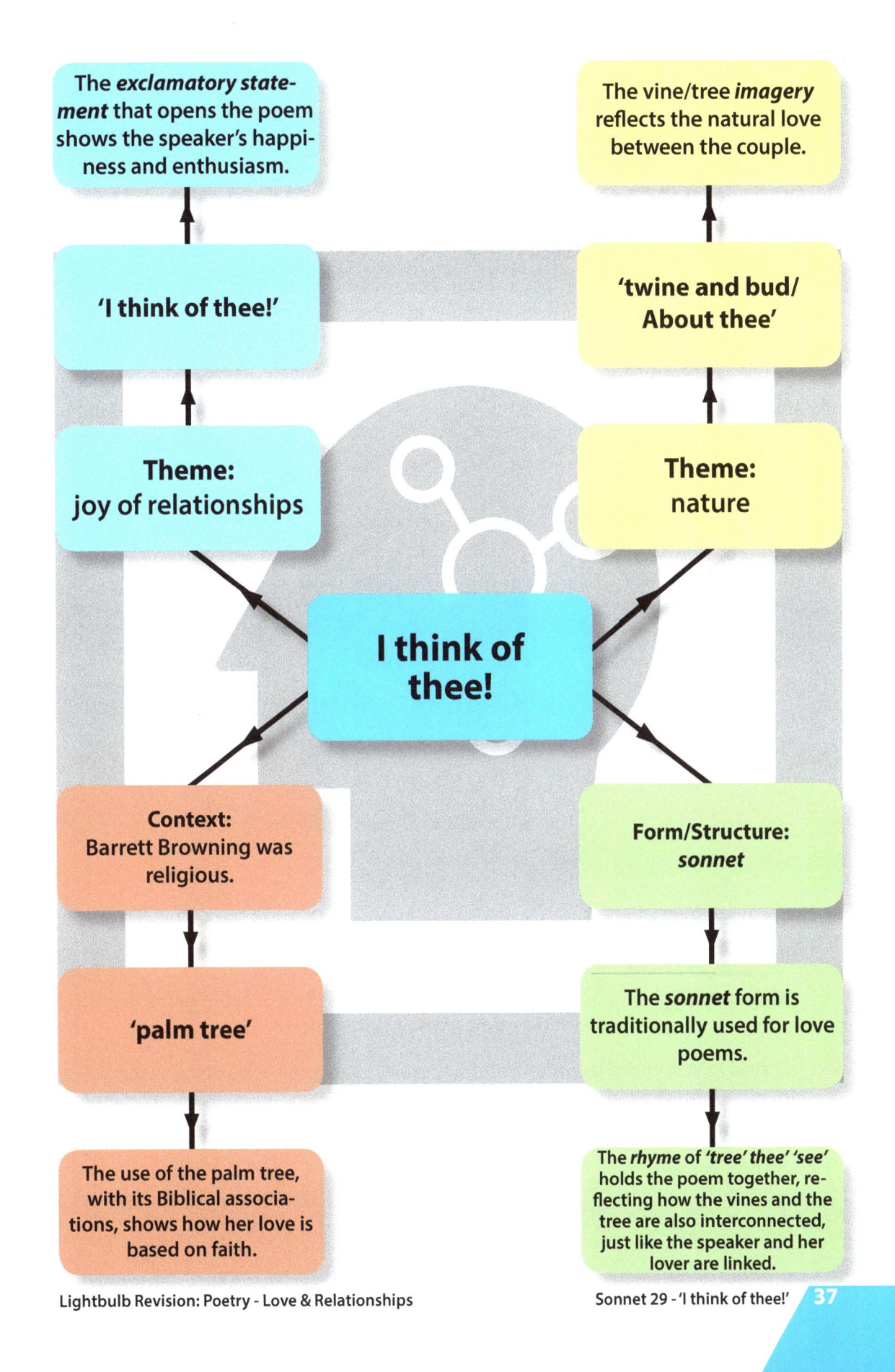

9 Letters from Yorkshire
Maura Dooley

Dooley explores the long-distance relationship between the speaker and her friend or partner in Yorkshire, examining their different lifestyles and their need to communicate with each other.

'the first lapwings return'

- The friend/partner in Yorkshire is connected with nature as he is in tune with the cyclical nature of migrating birds.
- It is a sign that winter is coming to an end, and so the poem opens with this positive *image* of the continuity of life and the hope of the regeneration that the spring brings.

'knuckles singing'

- **Personification** is used to show the delight the man feels in seeing the birds and also in writing to tell the speaker about it.
- **'Singing'** suggests celebration or praise which links to the sense of hope and positivity established with the sight of the birds in the previous line.
- The delight is in the communication; there is a sense that the man is excited, joyous, to be sharing his news with his friend.
- Singing is a form of communication; communication, in all its forms, is key to relationships.

'blank screen'

- **Contrast** is used to show the different life-styles. While the Yorkshire man is in the garden watching birds, the woman is linked to a computer screen.
- There is a sense of soullessness in the **adjective 'blank'**, suggesting that the world of computers is valueless and devoid (empty) of meaning (see Grade 9 Exploration Box).

'Is your life more real because you dig and sow?'

- The use of a question perhaps shows the doubt that the speaker has over her life choices.
- Perhaps there is a **tone** of regret in the question. The speaker is a long way from her home, living a very different lifestyle.

'pouring air and light into an envelope'

- The friend writes to the speaker who is far away in a city.
- This beautiful **metaphor** captures the positivity of this letter correspondence. The **metaphor** suggests the hope and brightness that the letter will bring and the pleasure the writer has in his letter. The **verb 'pouring'** indicates a fluidity, a smoothness, that again creates a pleasant **image**.
- The use of a nature **metaphor** connects the woman with the nature that she is missing out on.

'our souls tap out messages'

- This phrase is a celebration of the communication.
- **'Souls'** is deliberately used to show the intensely personal connection between them and the sense that the emails can easily travel **'icy miles'**. Even bleak weather cannot stop their communication.

Context

- Maura Dooley moved away from her roots and this experience of moving away from where one is born is a very common one, leaving many people with a feeling of regret or discontent.
- With the digital age of internet and emails, communication is becoming easier all the time. However, we are also perhaps becoming more disconnected with nature because of technology and there is an argument that digital communication (Facebook/emails/texts) means that we do not communicate properly with each other. These ideas are explored in the poem.

Form/Structure

- The lack of strict rhythm or rhyme reflects the ease and naturalness of her communication; the letter, the email and the headline show the importance of communication between people, from private individuals to a much wider public.
- This communication is also shown through the *enjambment* that connects most of the stanzas, for example, **'seeing the seasons/ turning'**. The *sibilance* of **'seeing'** **'seasons'** also helps create a soft gentle *rhythm* to the phrase, mirroring the smooth, cyclical changing of the seasons.

Comparison

- **Communication or lack of communication:** The Farmer's Bride/Neutral Tones
- **Being distanced from loved ones:** Before You Were Mine/Sonnet 29
- **Nature:** Follower/Love's Philosophy/Sonnet 29/Winter Swans

Grade 9 Exploration: Look at the poem in a different way

Is the man's life in Yorkshire more fulfilling than the woman's in London?

- **Yes:** *Contrast* is used to show the different life-styles. While the Yorkshire man is in the garden watching birds, the woman is linked to the **'blank screen'** of a computer. There is a sense of soullessness in the *adjective* **'blank'**, suggesting that the world of computers is valueless, empty, devoid of meaning.

- **No:** The computer simply represents another form of communication. The **'heartful of headlines'** suggests that she is writing for a newspaper which is a way of communicating with general public. Again there is a *contrast* between the private nature of the singular **'envelope'**- communication between two people- and the very public and prolific (plentiful) **'headlines'**. The poet is perhaps suggesting that all forms of communication are valid. The *metaphor* **'heartful'** suggests the emotional effort of writing for a newspaper and the emotional effect of reading the headlines. There is a sense that there is value to both the private letter and the public newspaper and therefore value to both lifestyles.

Letters from Yorkshire

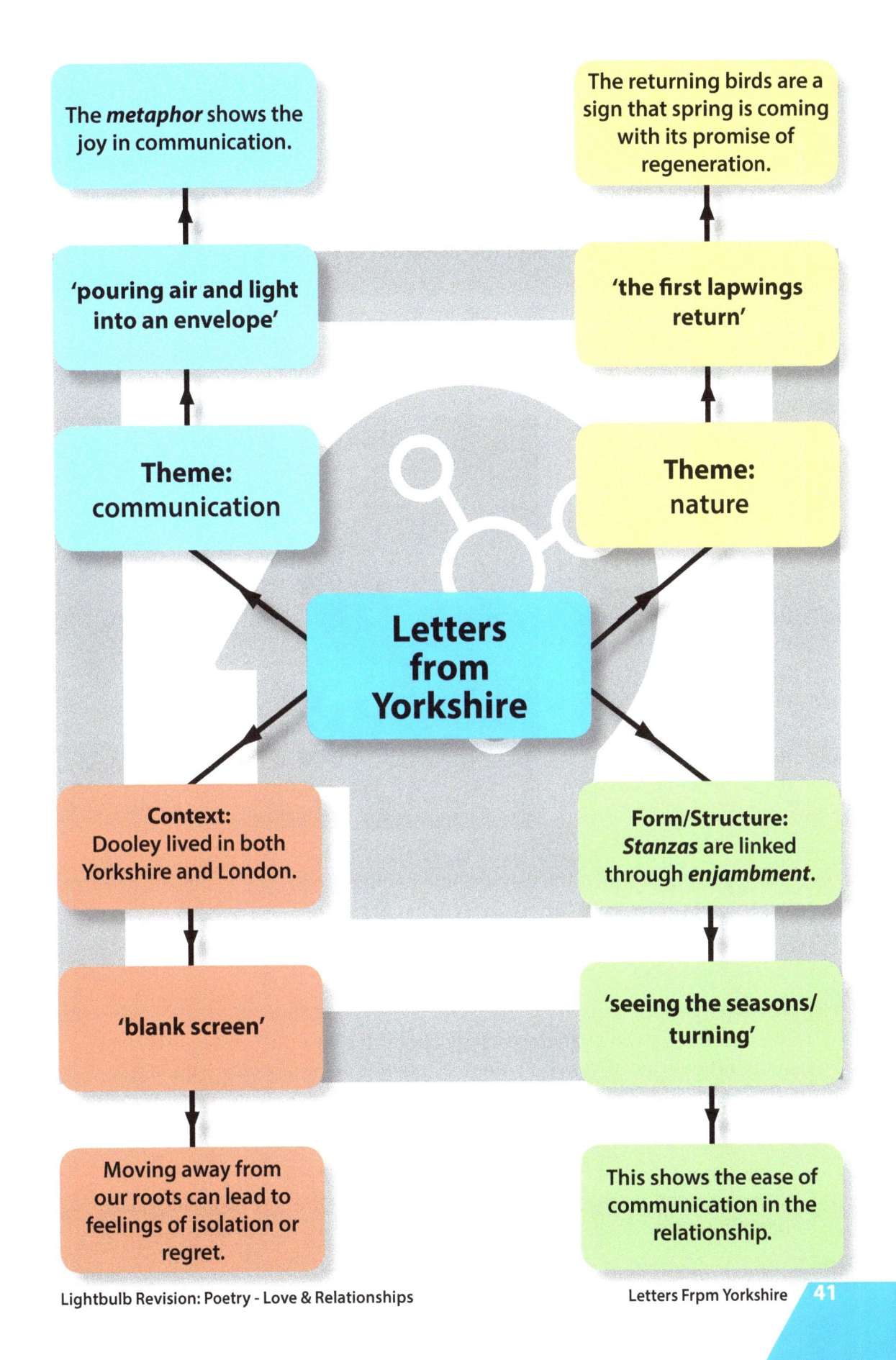

Theme: communication
- 'pouring air and light into an envelope'
  - The *metaphor* shows the joy in communication.

Theme: nature
- 'the first lapwings return'
  - The returning birds are a sign that spring is coming with its promise of regeneration.

Context: Dooley lived in both Yorkshire and London.
- 'blank screen'
  - Moving away from our roots can lead to feelings of isolation or regret.

Form/Structure: *Stanzas* are linked through *enjambment*.
- 'seeing the seasons/turning'
  - This shows the ease of communication in the relationship.

10 Walking Away
Cecil Day-Lewis

This poem captures the clear memory of a child walking away from his father at a school football match; the moment is used to highlight the natural separation of children from their parents and the emotions that this triggers.

'like a satellite/ Wrenched from its orbit'

- The speaker describes his son moving away from him.
- The **enjambment** highlights the physical and symbolic separation. It also emphasises the impact of the **verb** **'wrenched'** at the start of the next line. The **verb** is a painful one, reflecting the pain of the father as he realises his son is moving further away from him.
- The space **simile** shows the way a child gravitates to his or her parents, moving around the parent, staying close to him or her.

'drifting' 'scatter'

- The **vocabulary** shows an uncertainty about this parting. The boy isn't clear about his path away from his parent and seems vulnerable because of this.
- The parent is also unsure about letting him go. It is a time of flux (change) for both of them and the language captures this anxiety.
- **Enjambment** between these two lines reflects the hesitation and lack of a clear direct path as the boy moves away. These are the first, cautious steps of independence.

'gnaws'

- This memory is clearly one that has stayed with him as it **'gnaws'** at him.

- The **verb 'gnaws'** suggests a persistent action; this simple memory has never left him, showing its power and significance.

'Like a winged seed loosened from its parent stem'

- The nature **simile** emphasises that this parting is natural, part of the process all living things go through.

- There is a sense of comfort and acceptance in this to the man who sees his son growing up; he understands that his child has to fly off into the wider world, that it is an organic (natural) movement and not one that he could or should stop.

'God alone could perfectly show'

- This is a religious reference of God sending his son Jesus to earth, knowing that he would die. It shows a sense of sacrifice; part of a parent's role is to be selfless and to let go.

- The poet seems to find comfort in this thought. He uses nature and religion to accept his son's independence.

Context

- 'Walking Away' is a memory of the the poet's son's first day at school. Although published in the public form of a poem, it is a very private memory of a specific child and time. The speaker addresses his son, creating an intimate, emotional *tone* but it is an experience that almost every parent can relate to.

- Cecil Day-Lewis had a difficult relationship with his own father and there is a poignancy perhaps that he has such clear love and care of his own son.

- His father was a clergyman and the religious reference to God shows this influence.

Form/Structure

- 'Walking away' is used as a title and is also used in the last *stanza*, holding the memory and the poem tightly together.

- The use of the *present tense* allows us to understand how clear this memory still is, still very fresh in his mind. It gives the poem both a sense of immediacy and shows how the pain of that parting remains with him.

- *Fragmented speech*, indicated through the use of *dashes*, shows how the poet is pulling up the details of his memory. The *dashes* also create pauses which allow us to experience the emotions of the experience.

- The last lines bring us to a sense of conclusion; he has moved on from the pain of that day at school and shows acceptance.

Comparison

- **Memory:** Eden Rock/Before You Were Mine
- **Parent/child relationship:** Follower/Before You Were Mine/Mother, any distance

Grade 9 Exploration: Look at the poem in a different way

What does the ending show about how Day Lewis feels?

- The final *stanza* acts as a conclusion to the situation as the speaker states **'And love is proved in the letting go'**. The parent remembers his son parting from him and the pain that he felt, and yet has long come to terms with the need to allow children their freedom. The word **'proved'** means that the need for a parent to allow his child to separate from him has been shown to be true. This conclusion shows that Day-Lewis is acknowledging and accepting the universal truth of this.

- Alternatively, the *verb* **'gnaws'** shows a regret and pain rather than acceptance. There is a sense of persistence, at something nagging away.

- It is probable that there is a mixture of emotions felt by the poet.

Walking Away

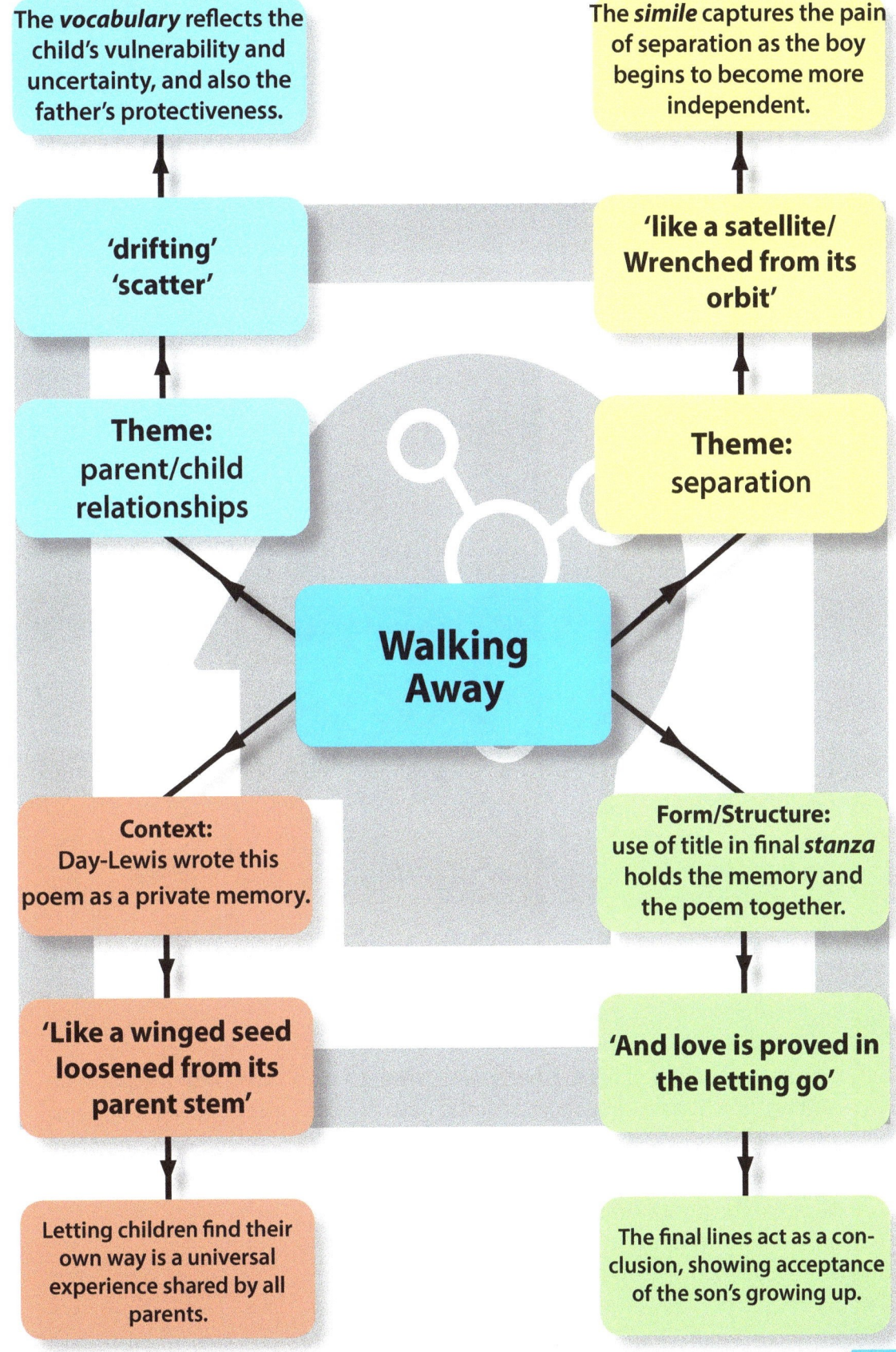

Theme: parent/child relationships

'drifting' 'scatter'

The *vocabulary* reflects the child's vulnerability and uncertainty, and also the father's protectiveness.

Theme: separation

'like a satellite/ Wrenched from its orbit'

The *simile* captures the pain of separation as the boy begins to become more independent.

Context: Day-Lewis wrote this poem as a private memory.

'Like a winged seed loosened from its parent stem'

Letting children find their own way is a universal experience shared by all parents.

Form/Structure: use of title in final *stanza* holds the memory and the poem together.

'And love is proved in the letting go'

The final lines act as a conclusion, showing acceptance of the son's growing up.

Lightbulb Revision: Poetry - Love & Relationships

11 Eden Rock
Charles Causley

The poet captures a real or imagined memory of a time when he was young, having a picnic with his parents. The poem is an affectionate exploration of the strong bonds between parents and children.

'Eden Rock'

- The place in the poem is a reference to the Garden of Eden, a place of perfect paradise. This suggests the idyllic nature of the place in Causley's childhood memory. There is a sense of nostalgia (remembering something fondly and a little sadly) here as the poet remembers a place that is gone. Just as Adam and Eve were forced to leave Eden, he is unable to return to his childhood and he only has memories of his now dead parents.

'hair, the colour of wheat, takes on the light'

- The natural colour of his mother's hair - **'wheat'** - works well with the natural setting which sits as a backdrop for the natural relationship between parents and child.
- It is a warm colour, helping to create a sense of a positive memory and a sense of the poet's affection for his parents.

'The sky whitens as if lit by three suns'

- In a prosaic (commonplace) poem full of everyday details, this is a moment which seems extraordinary as the sky changes colour.

- The light dominates the sky, drains it of colour- **'whitens'** it. This is a moment of an otherworldliness as the bright light suggests a vision of heaven.

- The *simile* **'as if lit by three suns'** links the three people: the mother, father and child. This highlights their togetherness and is a suggestion that the time has come for the speaker to join his parents in death. The brightness creates a positive *image* of death and what comes afterwards. It is also suggestive of the Holy Trinity (Father, Son, Holy Spirit) and reflects Causley's religious beliefs (see context box).

'Leisurely, /They beckon to me'

- **'Leisurely'** is a peaceful *adverb*, creating a sense of calm and peace. There is an impression that the poet is savouring (enjoying) his happy memory.

- It is comforting that the parents can still communicate with their child, showing that death does not break the bonds of parents and children.

- **'Leisurely'** could show the speaker's slow, steady approach to his own death. There is no panic or fear- just a leisurely acceptance of the passing of time.

- This slow, gentle pace is further created through the *enjambment* here, aided by the use of the comma which acts as a *caesura*.

'Crossing is not as hard as you might think'

- The parents' voices help create a vivid scene.
- Their words are encouraging and supportive, just as a parent is to a child.
- This shows the role of a parent: to help, to motivate. We see how the speaker's parents are there for him all through his life, right to the end. Their love and support is life-long.

Context

- Causley's memory of a perfect family picnic is one which many readers can relate to. It shows our tendency to look back at childhood memories with 'rose coloured spectacles' (see the memory as perfect) and not remember the negative aspects.

- Causley was religious and this is reflected in the poem. The clear images of his dead parents reflect his own certainty and belief in his faith: that, as a Christian, he will be re-born and see his parents again.

- Causley's father died when he was still a child so his view of him could well have been the idealised view of a child's perception of a parent.

Form/Structure

- There is a change from the regular **structure** of the poem at the end with the line **'I had not thought it would be like this'**. The final line is separated, as he moves from describing a memory to communicating his own thoughts. The separation reflects the separation of memory from real life.

- This final line is very simple. The **monosyllabic words** create a rather childish note of wonder and so creates a beautiful end to the poem. There is a sense of pleasure in that he will see his dead parents again as they were as a young couple and that the move to death will be a natural, easy move. This natural move is illustrated in the movement of the line away from the rest of the poem.

Comparison

- **Parent/Child relationships:** Follower/ Walking Away/ Before You Were Mine
- **Memory:** Walking Away/ Before You Were Mine
- **Separation:** Before You Were Mine / Mother, any distance

Grade 9 Exploration: Look at the poem in a different way

<u>Is this a real childhood memory of a time and place or is the poet dying and imagining his parents in heaven?</u>

- **Real memory:** the use of very precise details such as **'hair, the colour of wheat, takes on the light'** show how the poet has clear, realistic and precious memories. These details also work to create a very vivid picture for the reader- a snapshot of a time.

- **Parents in heaven:** Causley's use of **'light'** creates a sense of another, ethereal world. There is a sense that his parents are dead and his mother angelic.

- Maybe it is a mixture of the two, as our vision of the future is often influenced by our past experiences.

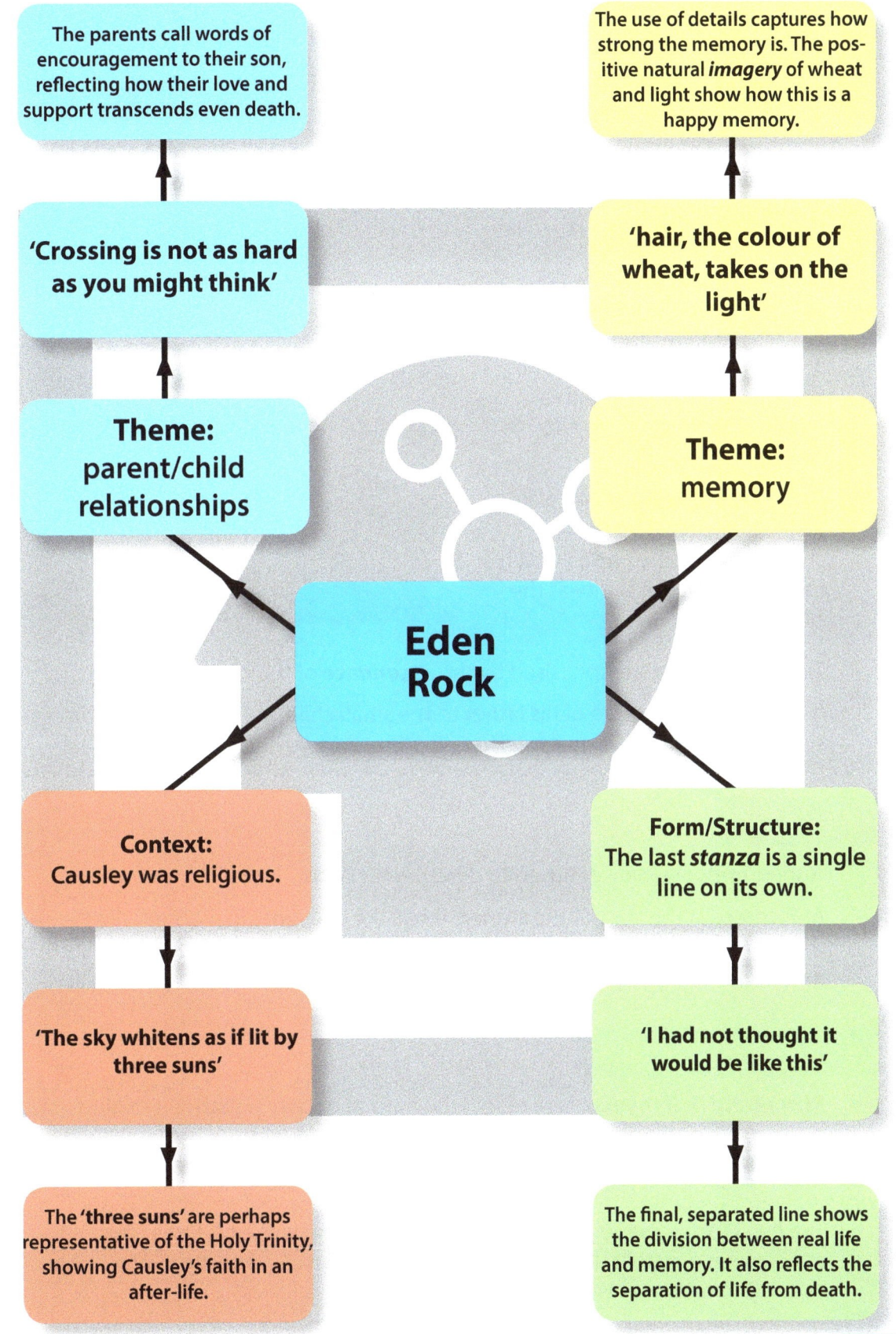

Eden Rock

Theme: parent/child relationships

'Crossing is not as hard as you might think'

The parents call words of encouragement to their son, reflecting how their love and support transcends even death.

Theme: memory

'hair, the colour of wheat, takes on the light'

The use of details captures how strong the memory is. The positive natural *imagery* of wheat and light show how this is a happy memory.

Context: Causley was religious.

'The sky whitens as if lit by three suns'

The **'three suns'** are perhaps representative of the Holy Trinity, showing Causley's faith in an after-life.

Form/Structure: The last *stanza* is a single line on its own.

'I had not thought it would be like this'

The final, separated line shows the division between real life and memory. It also reflects the separation of life from death.

Lightbulb Revision: Poetry - Love & Relationships

12 Follower
Seamus Heaney

Heaney writes a moving tribute to his farmer father, revealing a respect for the man and his work. The poem also tracks the passing of time and how relationships naturally change.

'His shoulders globed like a full sail strung'

- This **simile** uses nautical terminology to describe his father as physically impressive and strong.
- It suggests stateliness and also a sense of grace. There is a smoothness to the **image** which reflects his natural ability at the ploughing.
- This smoothness is emphasised by the **assonance** of the 'o' sound.
- It also suggests the size of his father to the small child, looking up at his impressive father, as large as a full sail. There is a **tone** of awe here.

'An expert.'

- A short **minor** sentence is used to describe his father.
- As it comes at the start of the **stanza**, it has the effect of highlighting the father's prowess at ploughing. There is a very clear confidence about the statement and a **tone** of admiration and respect for his father's indisputable skill.

'sod/plod' 'wake/back'

- **Rhyme** and **half rhymes** here reflect the natural pace of his father working.
- The **half rhymes** give the poem a natural feel as it is not uniform. This illustrates the irregular movements of pulling a plough.
- The **half rhyme** also suggests that the son wants to be like his father but cannot be; he is a near fit but not a proper one. He doesn't perfectly match but he does try to emulate his father.

'I stumbled in his hob-nailed wake'

- Stanza 4 moves from the description of the father to a focus on the son, the narrator.

- **'Stumbled'** is a clumsy **verb**, showing the boy was far from an expert in the fields.

- The **alliteration** of the 'b' sounds here also capture this clumsiness.

- **'Wake'** picks up the nautical **imagery** of the sail in stanza 1. Heaney extends this **image** of the boat with the boy following in the **'wake'** (a track through the waves left by a boat). He is trying to keep up and to be like his father, but fails.

'I was a nuisance, tripping, falling/Yapping always'

- There is a clear **statement** here that the boy knew he was in his father's way, a hindrance and not a help to his father's work.

- The **asyndetic list** here crowds the **verbs** together, emphasising how much of a pain he was being.

'It is my father who keeps stumbling/ Behind me, and will not go away'

- The shift in **tenses** from past to present show that the time has changed.

- The relationship has also changed; the earlier **tone** of admiration has changed to a **tone** of irritation. His father has become the clumsy, incompetent one causing a nuisance to the son.

- The **enjambment** emphasises the clumsiness of the father and the impatience of the son.

- Heaney allows us to see how there is a natural, and painful, shift from the hero worship children show their parents to the realisation that parents are just human and therefore frail.

Context

- Heaney grew up in rural Ireland and the use of terminology such as **'shafts'** and **'furrow'** shows he is very familiar with the situation and place that he is describing.
- This is a personal poem; Heaney lived on his father's farm so this is a memory that has stayed with him.
- Families in rural Ireland in the twentieth century were close-knit and Heaney would be expected to care for his aging parents.
- It is also a universal experience; we almost all have to experience our parents ageing and the changes that brings.

Form/Structure

- The first three *stanzas* focus entirely on the father, showing the poet's admiration of his skill.
- The focus then shifts to the poet's perspective as a boy and in the final *stanza* there is a *volta* with the word **'but'** as the poet reflects on the change in their roles and ends with the acknowledgement that it is his father who is now dependent on him.

Comparison

- **Parent/child relationships:** Walking Away/Mother, any distance /Before You Were Mine
- **Hero worship:** Climbing my Grandfather/Before You Were Mine
- **Time changing relationships:** Mother, any distance/Walking Away
- **Nature:** Letters from Yorkshire

Grade 9 Exploration: Look at the poem in a different way

What does 'follower' mean?

- Heaney feels guilty that he is not actually a follower: he has not continued in his father's job of ploughing. He is disappointed in himself that he had not followed or lived up to his father's magnificent example.
- Alternatively, 'Follower' refers to his father; it is his old, frail father who follows his son, showing that relationships shift with age.
- Yet another interpretation is that 'Follower' could suggest the way we, as humans, follow the patterns of life. From dependent child, to strong independent adult, to dependent adult.

Follower

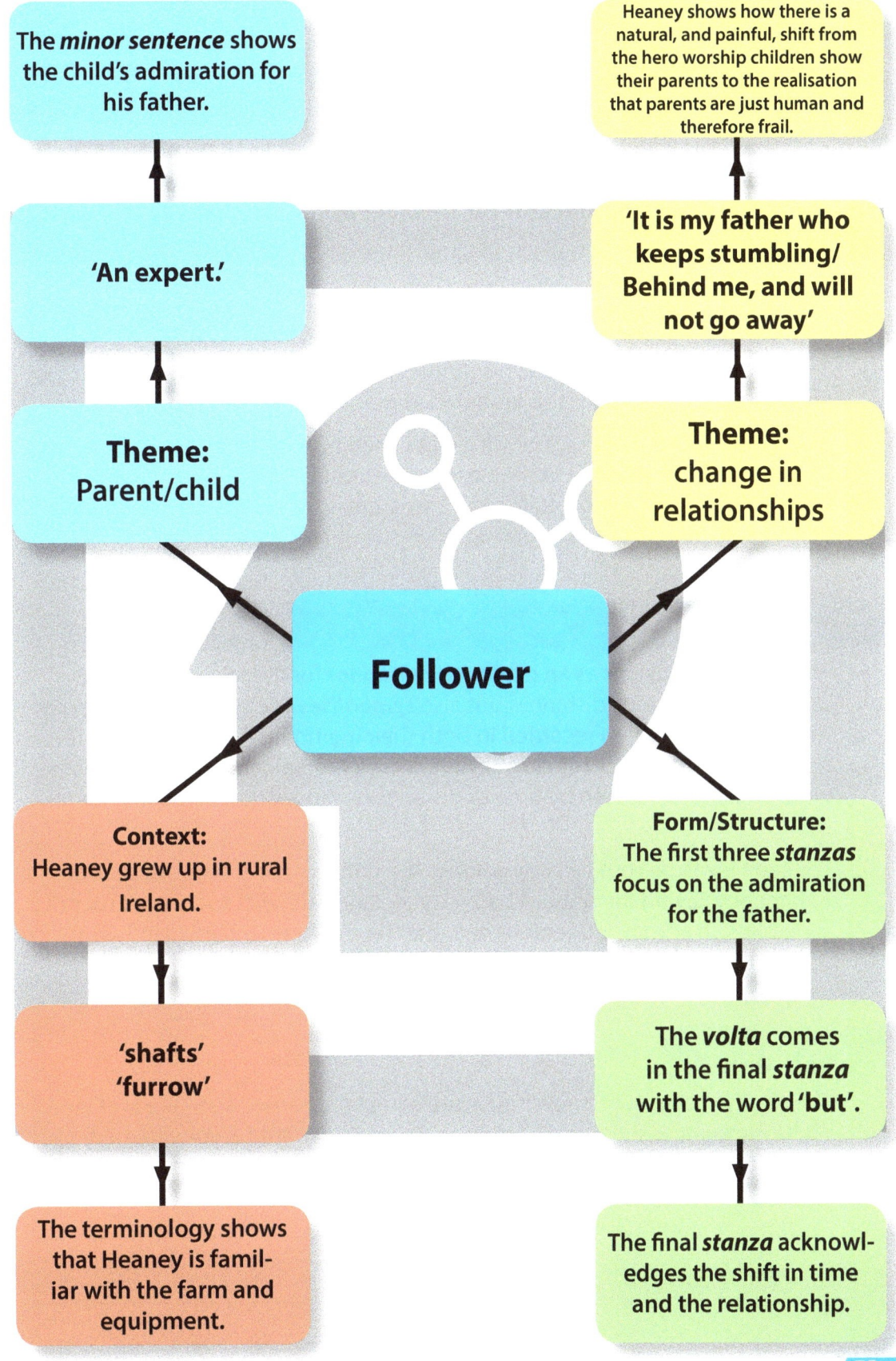

Theme: Parent/child

'An expert.'

The *minor sentence* shows the child's admiration for his father.

Theme: change in relationships

'It is my father who keeps stumbling/ Behind me, and will not go away'

Heaney shows how there is a natural, and painful, shift from the hero worship children show their parents to the realisation that parents are just human and therefore frail.

Context: Heaney grew up in rural Ireland.

'shafts' 'furrow'

The terminology shows that Heaney is familiar with the farm and equipment.

Form/Structure: The first three *stanzas* focus on the admiration for the father.

The *volta* comes in the final *stanza* with the word '**but**'.

The final *stanza* acknowledges the shift in time and the relationship.

Lightbulb Revision: Poetry - Love & Relationships

Follower 53

13 Mother, any distance
Simon Armitage

Armitage explores a young man's bond with his mother as they measure for furnishings in his new home. The poem affectionately examines the relationship between mother and son, and how this changes as the son takes a step towards independence.

'Mother, any distance'

- The speaker directly addresses his mother, allowing the reader to listen to the speaker's thoughts about this landmark day.
- The title suggests that the son will always need his mother and be connected to her. Indeed, at no point in the poem is the connection between the two severed; they both hold onto the tape measure as he climbs up through the house, reflecting the continuous bond of parent and child.

'zero-end... of tape... , recording length...unreeling years'

- The tape measure acts as an **extended metaphor** for the relationship. The tape measure records distances but also **symbolises** the years of shared experiences that have been recorded in both their memories. The tape measure, held by by each of them at either end, shows the connection between them which will not be broken by time or distance because of these shared memories.
- The tape measure could also **symbolise** the umbilical cord that ties a mother to her baby, giving the unborn baby oxygen and nutrients to survive. There is perhaps an acknowledgement here that his mother is essential to him still: her continued love and help are an important part of his independence.

'acres' 'prairies'

- The empty spaces in the new house are compared to vast open areas of land. These **metaphors** suggest that the speaker feels daunted (overwhelmed) by the unfamiliar unknown space. He is not yet completely independent.

'Anchor.'

- The single word sentence emphasises the importance of his mother as the person that holds steady in his life, the person that he can always rely on. She is a constant in his life.

'centimetres' 'inch'

- The son and mother use different ways of measuring, showing the difference in approach created by the age gap.

- It could also show how the son needs his independence; their measurements are inherently (essentially) different as the same distance will be one figure in centimeters and another in inches.

- There is a sense of a clash here, an incompatibility (incapable of working together). Here, the poet shows the change in their relationship as the son chooses his own way of recording and living his life.

'recording' 'reporting' 'space walk'

- The mother and the tape measure are imposing restrictions and rules.

- These **verbs** of control- **'recording'** and **'reporting'** - **contrast** with the son's **'space walk'** which is a humorous **image** showing the son bounding free from even that most basic of rules, that of gravity.

- **'Space walk'** also allows us to imagine the son left free to explore the whole universe: bounding through unchartered (unmapped) territory, reflecting that his life free from parental control will be an exciting, unknown adventure.

'Kite.' 'Fall or fly'

- At the end, the poet returns to an earlier **image** of him being a kite, flying free as he reaches the next stage of independence.

- The way Armitage ends the poem by referencing the earlier **image** shows the family connection holding true right to the end and creates a comforting feel that the mother will always be there for her son.

Context

- Modern parents encourage their children to value independence and move out of the family home and the mother in this poem is clearly doing this.
- The poem comes from a collection inspired from a party game where players have to talk about their lives in the time it takes for a match to burn. There is a sense of a snapshot of a moment in the speaker's life in the poem.

Form/Structure

- The **structure** reflects the idea of breaking free.
- The poem starts with the semblance (appearance) of a formal **sonnet** structure with a **rhyming couplet 'doors/floors'** and a four line verse.
- By the end, the final **stanza** is five lines long with irregular meter, showing the son stepping outside parental limits and choosing his own path.
- However, the poem finishes with another **rhyming couplet 'sky/fly'**, implying that the mother and son are still connected; despite the relationship inevitably changing, they will still be close.

Comparison

- **Changing relationships:** Follower/Walking Away/Mother, any distance
- **Respect/love for older family member:** Climbing my Grandfather/Before You Were Mine/Follower

Grade 9 Exploration: Look at the poem in a different way

Is the poet's relationship with his mother becoming difficult?

- **Yes:** The **verb 'pinch'** reflects the way his mother holds onto the tape measure to the very last inch. It illustrates the tightness with which his mother holds on, possibly too tight. **'Pinch'** has connotations with being uncomfortable, even painful; maybe his mother is desperately trying to hold on to her son leaving the nest and this is causing tension.
- **No:** **'Mother, any distance'** suggests that the son will always need his mother and be connected to her. At no point in the poem is the connection between the two severed; they both hold onto the tape measure no matter how high he climbs away from her. The affectionate **tone** to this poem also shows a close relationship.

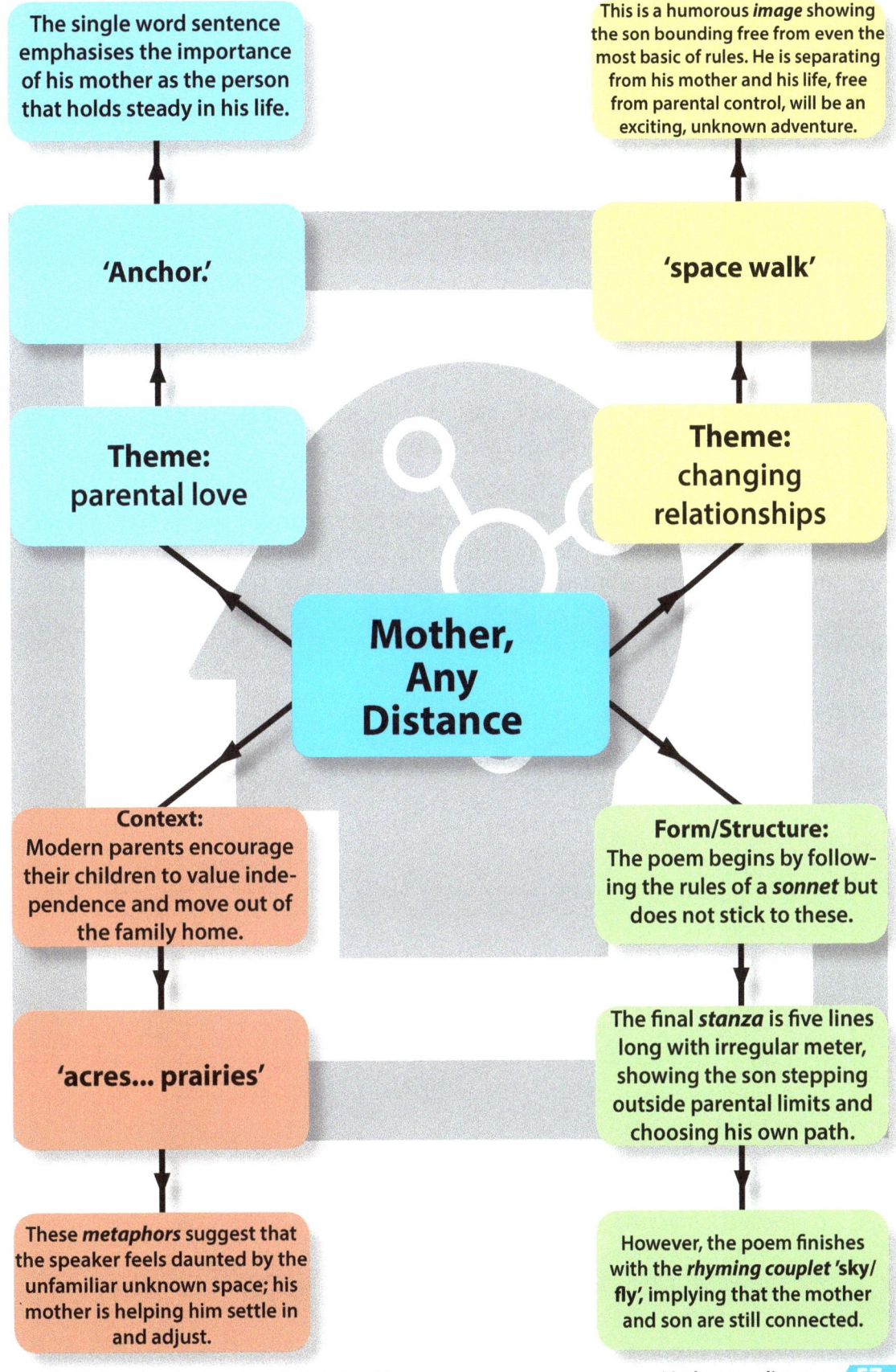

Mother, Any Distance

'Anchor.'
— The single word sentence emphasises the importance of his mother as the person that holds steady in his life.

Theme: parental love

'space walk'
— This is a humorous *image* showing the son bounding free from even the most basic of rules. He is separating from his mother and his life, free from parental control, will be an exciting, unknown adventure.

Theme: changing relationships

Context: Modern parents encourage their children to value independence and move out of the family home.

'acres… prairies'
— These *metaphors* suggest that the speaker feels daunted by the unfamiliar unknown space; his mother is helping him settle in and adjust.

Form/Structure: The poem begins by following the rules of a *sonnet* but does not stick to these.

The final *stanza* is five lines long with irregular meter, showing the son stepping outside parental limits and choosing his own path.

However, the poem finishes with the *rhyming couplet* 'sky/fly', implying that the mother and son are still connected.

Lightbulb Revision: Poetry - Love & Relationships

14 Before You Were Mine
Carol Ann Duffy

Duffy imagines her mother's life and character as a young woman, before she became a mother, and in doing so explores the mother-daughter relationship with all its layers of love and possessiveness.

'Before you were mine'

- This **repeated** phrase is used in the title, second stanza and final line. This **repetition** shows the deep bond between the mother and daughter.

- The **personal pronoun 'mine'** shows how the girl sees her mother as belonging to her, inextricably (impossible to separate) connected.

- A child does indeed possess a mother's life: dominates it and controls it by its need to be cared for and the fierce nature of maternal love. Yet the speaker shows a desire to extend their relationship by wishing to know and see her mother as a young woman.

'high-heeled red shoes'

- Duffy uses specific detail to capture her mother's character; the red suggests a brightness and a lack of caution and the high-heels suggests frivolity (fun) and glamour.

- By the time Duffy is a girl, these shoes are **'relics'**. They are consigned (belong) to a past that Duffy can never be part of as the mother has no need to wear such frivolous shoes. This shows how responsibilities alter us.

'Your polka-dot dress blows round your legs. Marilyn'

- The speaker describes her mother as a young woman whose dress is blowing round her legs, like the famous photo of Marilyn Monroe, a 50s film star. The *image* is one of freedom and flirtatiousness, showing how the mother's life was once very different.
- It is possible that the speaker is looking at an old photograph of her mother, or even remembering looking as a child at the photograph. However, the use of the *present tense* suggests that this is an event happening now. This shows the power of memories, both real and imagined.
- We do question the accuracy of the memories, though, as the speaker was never there with her mother; she is imagining her mother rather than remembering her.

'Cha cha cha!'

- Yet her mother's character is not completely changed as her mother used to dance with her on the way home from church.
- The final *stanza* opens with the quick sounding, *monosyllabic* words that vividly create a sense of fun and movement and reinforce her mother's vitality.
- Her mother danced as a young single woman but still dances with her daughter, suggesting a fun-loving character who still bends the rules. As a teenager, she was the last one home from the night out but, as a mother, she is also dancing on the way home from mass.

'yell' 'clatter'

- Duffy uses *onomatopoeic* sounds to show the contrast between her mother's light, tripping footsteps as she came home from the dance hall with the demanding, unpleasant sound of the baby shouting.
- Duffy acknowledges how her birth must have irrevocably (can't be changed) altered her mother's lifestyle.

'sparkle and waltz and laugh'

- The *sydentic list* builds up a positive *image* of her mother as Duffy clearly admires her mother and almost envies her.
- The *verbs* in their *present tense* form imply that the mother is still vivacious (lively) and glamorous. However, then the final phrase **'before you were mine'** brings the young woman to the position of mother where she has to put herself last and her daughter first, acknowledging the bond and responsibility a child brings.

Context

- The reference to Marilyn Monroe takes us back to the 1950s when Marilyn Monroe, the Hollywood actress, was a top celebrity.
- The Scottish *dialect* of **'Ma'** also connects the poem with a place: Glasgow, Scotland, where Duffy was born.
- There is perhaps a sense of Duffy's Catholic upbringing in the reference to **'mass'** and also the phrase **'wrong pavement'**, relating to the moral code of **'right'** and **'wrong'** taught to her as a child. Alternatively, perhaps the phrase suggests the different directions her life went; the **'right pavement'** as a girl in Scotland and then the **'wrong pavement'** as she moved to England when her daughter (the poet talking) was six years old.

Form/Structure

- The persona moves constantly between memories, both real and imagined. The use of *present tense* gives the memories an immediacy and vivacity (liveliness) that is compelling, and also helps weave the strong relationship between the mother and daughter firmly together.
- The *repetition* of the phrase **'Before you were mine'** connects the *stanzas*. The poem ends with this phrase, showing the finality of the end of the mother's young, carefree life. By the end of the poem, she is rooted in her role as mother.

Comparison

- **Parent/Child relationships:** Follower/Walking Away/Mother, any distance
- **Memory:** Walking Away/Follower
- **Separation:** Before You Were Mine/Mother, any distance

Grade 9 Exploration: Look at the poem in a different way

How does the poet feel towards her mother?

- Love: The conversational *tone* and *direct address* of **'whose small bites on your neck, sweetheart?'** create an intimate feel, as does the endearment **'sweetheart'**. The speaker loves her mother and wants to know her history, probing the past as she tries to extend her relationship and connect further with her mother.
- Regret: The daughter regrets that she will never know her mother as the young carefree girl and so eagerly questions her to learn her history second hand.
- Jealousy: Alternatively, the phrase could suggest jealousy as the persona's need for her mother to share everything, even her past, shows a real possessiveness.
- Perhaps a mixture of all these, reflecting the many layers of the relationship.

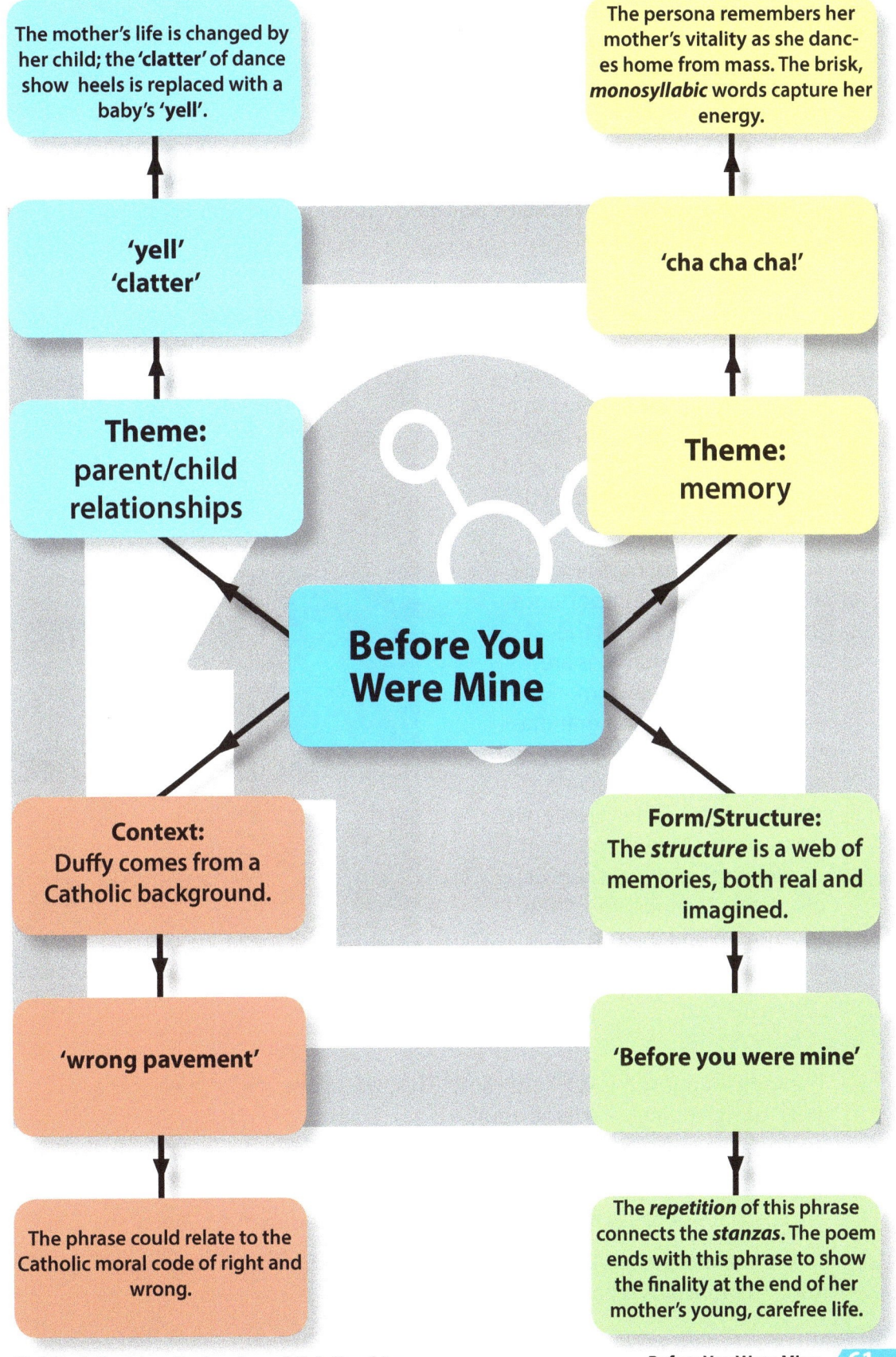

Before You Were Mine

Theme: parent/child relationships

'yell'
'clatter'

The mother's life is changed by her child; the **'clatter'** of dance show heels is replaced with a baby's **'yell'**.

Theme: memory

'cha cha cha!'

The persona remembers her mother's vitality as she dances home from mass. The brisk, *monosyllabic* words capture her energy.

Context:
Duffy comes from a Catholic background.

'wrong pavement'

The phrase could relate to the Catholic moral code of right and wrong.

Form/Structure:
The *structure* is a web of memories, both real and imagined.

'Before you were mine'

The *repetition* of this phrase connects the *stanzas*. The poem ends with this phrase to show the finality at the end of her mother's young, carefree life.

Lightbulb Revision: Poetry - Love & Relationships

Before You Were Mine 61

15 Climbing My Grandfather
Andrew Waterhouse

Waterhouse uses the *extended metaphor* of mountaineering to describe the speaker's memories of clambering over his grandfather as a child. This is a poem which shows the affectionate bond between the two generations.

'Climbing My Grandfather'

- The title is humorous and engaging, establishing the **metaphor** of his grandfather being a mountain. The size of the man shows the young child's view of him, that he is so large as to be a mountain of a man.

- The mountain **metaphor** could also **symbolise** the importance the grandfather had in the speaker's life. Mountains are fixed and notable landmarks; this echoes the role of the grandfather and reminds the reader how important the older people in our families are. They are significant, constant figures as we grow up, unlike nursery teachers or playground friends, and often have great influence on us.

'trying' 'pull'

- The **verbs** suggest this is a hard climb. This would actually be the case for a small boy climbing up a large adult.

- The **verbs** could also indicate that the speaker is trying to remember a dead relative and finding the process of dredging through his memories a difficult one, perhaps because it's so long ago and the memories have faded.

- Or the **verbs** could show us that getting to know someone and to form significant relationships is hard work.

'earth-stained hand'

- Waterhouse uses precise details to give us clues about the man's personality and lifestyle. Here, we have an impression of a man who worked outside, perhaps a manual labourer, perhaps a farmer, and so someone who worked hard. Alternatively, perhaps he loved gardening as a hobby and so was someone who was attuned (connected) to nature.

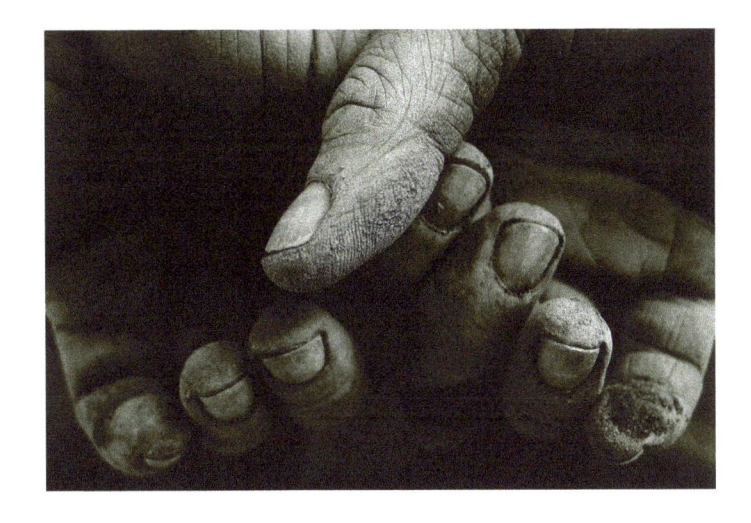

- The details also show a closeness between the old man and the young boy; the man allows his grandchild such intimate (close) access and scrutiny of his body at close quarters.

'firm shoulder' 'smiling mouth'

- As the child ascends, Waterhouse presents a range of positive **images**, showing a sense of respect for this man and using a **tone** of admiration.

'the slow pulse of his good heart'

- The poem ends with the boy nestling up to his grandfather and listening to his heartbeat.

- The physical closeness reflects the emotional closeness. There is no doubting the affection between the two as he is so close he can feel his grandfather's heart beating. The **adjective 'good'** is the culmination (conclusion) of all the positivity built up in the poem about the grandfather; it clearly states that this grandfather was a man worthy of love and respect.

- The **monosyllabic** words and **long vowel sounds** capture the sense of the boy resting after the exhausting climb, perhaps suggesting getting to know someone well takes determination and effort. Yet the message of the poem is that this effort is worth it.

Context

- Andrew Waterhouse was a committed environmentalist and his love of nature is reflected in the **metaphor** of a mountain.
- It is a personal memory but explores a universal experience.

Form/Structure

- The poem is written as one **stanza** without a break, showing the continuous action of the boy climbing up the bulk of his grandfather.
- **'First… on…. at… then'**: The poet uses **prepositions** to show the progression of the child as he crawls over the old man. The **prepositions** are also a **structural** device to move the reader through the process of getting to see the grandfather's body and to see glimpses of his personality.
- The poem ends with the completion of the boy's climb; it is a positive ending showing the affection between the two.

Comparison

- **Parent/child relationships:** Walking Away/Mother, any distance/Before You Were Mine
- **Hero worship:** Follower/Before You Were Mine
- **Time changing relationships:** Mother, any distance/Walking Away

Grade 9 Exploration: Look at the poem in a different way

Is there a wholly (completely) positive view of relationships?

Positive: As the child ascends, Waterhouse presents range of positive **images** such as **'firm shoulder…smiling mouth'**, showing a sense of respect for this man and using a **tone** of admiration.

Negative: Possibly the drop down seems enormous to the small boy as he says **'not looking down/for climbing has its dangers'**. It could also suggest the dangers of trying to bring back memories; to remember his grandfather is to remember the grief of his death, and this is dangerous and hurtful. The speaker is perhaps remembering his dead grandfather but struggles to remember him. This lack of clear memory is painful and perhaps upsets him. Perhaps the poet is suggesting that getting to know someone is in itself a dangerous exercise as who knows what you will discover. Also, by getting close to someone can make you vulnerable if they let you down or don't love you back or leave you. Forming connections and relationships can be treacherous.

Climbing My Grandfather

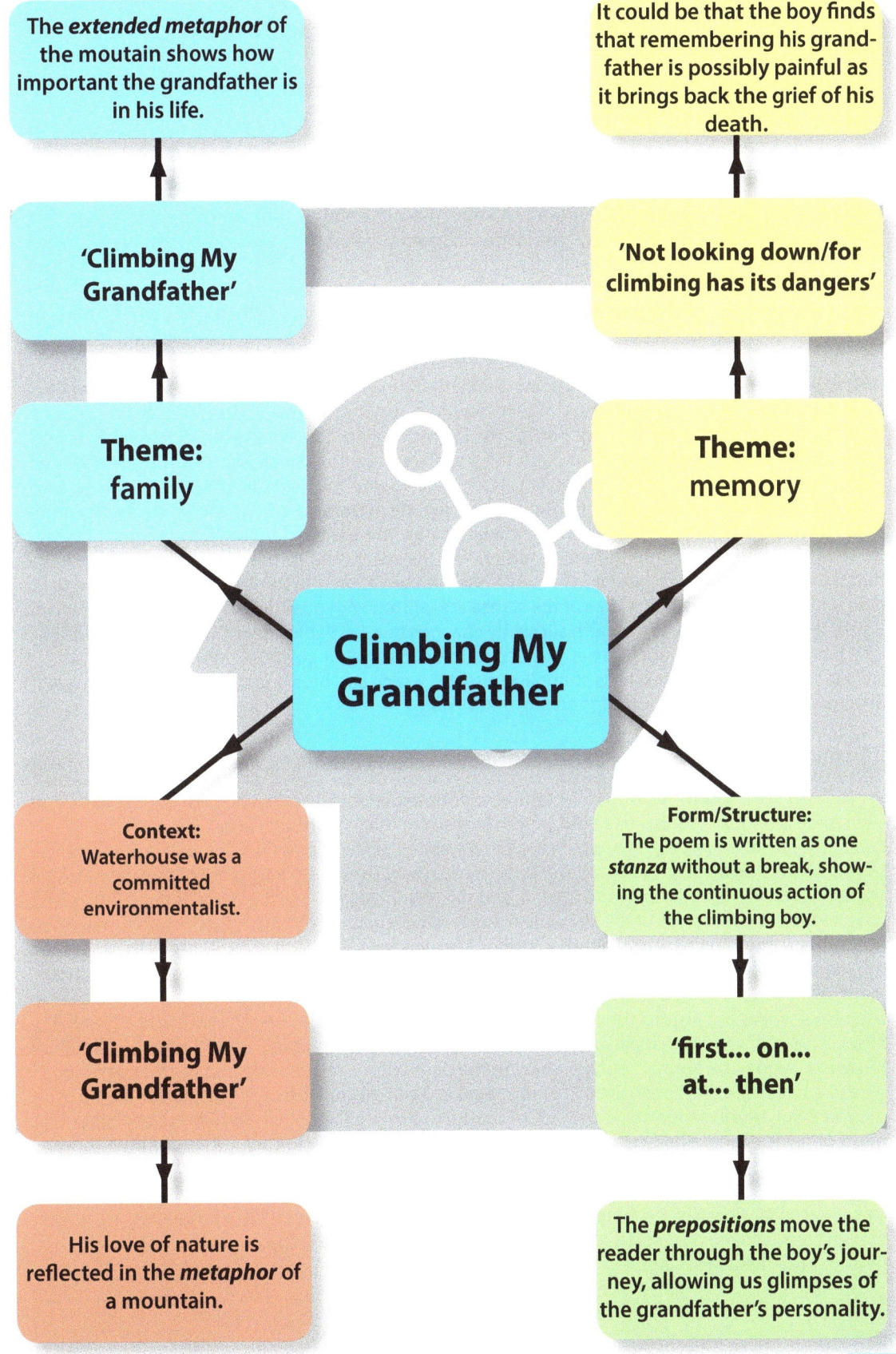

Theme: family → 'Climbing My Grandfather' → The *extended metaphor* of the mountain shows how important the grandfather is in his life.

Theme: memory → 'Not looking down/for climbing has its dangers' → It could be that the boy finds that remembering his grandfather is possibly painful as it brings back the grief of his death.

Context: Waterhouse was a committed environmentalist. → 'Climbing My Grandfather' → His love of nature is reflected in the *metaphor* of a mountain.

Form/Structure: The poem is written as one *stanza* without a break, showing the continuous action of the climbing boy. → 'first... on... at... then' → The *prepositions* move the reader through the boy's journey, allowing us glimpses of the grandfather's personality.

Lightbulb Revision: Poetry - Love & Relationships

End of a relationship: Question & Answer

Compare how the end of relationships are presented in 'Neutral Tones' and 'When We Two Parted'.

☑ **Make the point that both poets show us the pain triggered by the end of a relationship**

'Neutral Tones' and 'When We Two Parted' both document the end of a relationship and the pain that this brings. In 'Neutral Tones', Hardy shares with us a memory that shows the death of love, focusing on the negative emotions that are experienced at this time as he describes his lover's smile **'like an ominous bird a-wing…'** The *simile* compares the lover's grin to a prophetic bird of doom, as an omen that forecasts the end of their relationship. The *ellipsis* marks a turning point in the poem as the poet finishes his memory, yet it could also suggest that the memory lingers on in the poet's mind. It could well be a real memory as Hardy's first marriage was an unhappy one and his difficult relationships with women are reflected here in this poem. Similarly, Bryon also shares with the reader the death of a relationship as he and his lover separate. He is writing about a real event, documenting the end of his affair with Lady Webster, who left him for the Duke of Wellington. We see the increased distance between the speaker and his lover through the line **'Pale grew thy cheek and cold/Colder thy kiss'**. Combined with the word **'chill'** in *stanza* 2, Byron uses a *semantic field* that creates a lack of warmth, reflecting the bleak nature of his suffering, and we see the *metaphorical* cooling of the relationship as the woman emotionally withdraws from the relationship and the passions of their love fade. The word **'cold'** is *repeated* to highlight the shock and grief of the speaker while the *enjambment* also ensures that the second **'colder'** at the start of the line hits with extra force. Bryon uses *accentual verse* to reflect his pain here: the first 4 lines of the stanza are written with precise regularity of 5 syllables and 2 stressed syllables. Here, the pattern suddenly changes to a 6 syllable line with 3 stressed syllables which breaks the pattern and startles the reader. This sudden change in the *rhythm* reflects the speaker's trauma, almost as if he is stumbling over his words and breaking down. Both poets leave us in no doubt that these relationships are beyond saving.

☑ **Move to the point that both poets use the senses to show us the end of a relationship**

Senses are used by both poets to reflect the emotions experienced at the end of relationships. Hardy uses colour *imagery* to show us a cold, barren landscape that is **'ash'** and **'grey'**. The dull colours reflect the speaker's relationship, which has been washed of life or emotion. The **'ash'** tree has hints of a fire that has burnt out, leaving nothing but dust. It *symbolises* the burning out of passion as love is traditionally linked to heat but here the fire, and the relationship, is burnt out and is dead. This is also reflected in the description of the sky with its white **'God-curst sun'**, creating an incredibly negative atmosphere through the sun's unnatural colour. We wonder whether the couple are being punished by God in the failure of their relationship; Hardy's writings consistently explore this sense of punishment, of an unfeeling, cold divine presence which treats humans harshly. Byron does not use colours and visual senses but instead uses aural senses. His lover has found someone else and the gossipy news of his lost love's new affair sounds like a **'knell'** in the speaker's ear. The *metaphor* of a **'knell in mine ear'** suggests a funeral bell, *symbolising* the death of the relationship and the *monosyllabic* phrase emphasises the leaden despair of the speaker. The bell *contrasts* with the earlier theme of silence; Byron is using sound, and the lack of sound, to explore the dissolving of his relationship. This *motif* of silence could signify that the lovers have nothing left to say to each other. Communication between them has broken down as feelings have died out although, alternatively, the silence could suggest that, far from emotionless, the poet is almost speechless with grief. Another way that the silence is used is to emphasise that the love is clandestine and must be shrouded in secrecy. The sense of silence reflects the rigid social mores (conventions) of the time that Byron was writing in and the need to keep the affair secret.

☑ Make the point that both poets show us a range of emotions

Both poets convey the pain of the end of a relationship yet this is not the only emotion that a break-up brings. Hardy's language choices clearly reveals his bitterness with the **statement** that **'love deceives'**, showing his bitter disillusionment with love and suggesting that he is angry, blaming his partner for the break-up. This emotion is also evident in 'When We Two Parted' as there is anger here as well at the lack of fidelity and the destruction of trust, with Byron accusing his ex-mistress that **'thy vows are all broken'**. The **tone** is accusatory; he pins the blame on his lover with a **declarative statement** of how she has broken her promises. Byron uses the language of marriage to show how special their love was, yet this also highlights how deeply she has betrayed him. This is a very personal poem in that the speaker directly addresses his lover **'thy'** throughout, creating an intimate feel, as if we are eavesdropping on a very personal conversation. The lack of names suggests that Byron was writing about his own experience and hiding his lover's name was a way of protecting her. Yet the lack of names also gives this poem a universal appeal as any reader who has lost a lover can relate to the enduring pain and complexities of emotions. This complexity of emotions is seen in the words **'shame'** and **'rue'**, reflecting how the speaker feels embarrassment and regret. This could be very different from Hardy's stance; interestingly, it is arguable that Hardy feels very little emotion at all at the end of his relationship. The use of commas in the final **stanza** creates a disjointed, awkward pace which reflects the speaker's disconnection with the situation. The **anaphora** in the last stanza of **'and' 'and'** with **monosyllabic** words creates a heavy, defeated **tone** at the end. Hardy ends his poem with this dull, lifeless **rhythm** to perhaps express his own lack of emotion about the relationship.

☑ Finish with the point that both poets use structure to explore the end of a relationship

Hardy and Byron use **structure** to reflect ideas and emotions associated with the end of a relationship; they both use **tenses** to show us how it is very difficult to put a failed relationship behind us. In 'Neutral Tones', the last **stanza** is in the **present tense**, suggesting that the memory is fresh in his mind and that he revisits it. This is also encapsulated (shown) by the **circular structure**; the poem begins and ends with the pond, suggesting how the event has influenced his life. Like the still water of the pond does not move, he also has not moved on; the **circular structure** shows that he cannot escape this unhappy memory. Similarly, the use of **tenses** help structure Byron's poem: the 4 stanzas move from **past tense**, to the **present tense**, to the **future conditional tense** 'if I should meet thee'. This suggests the extended pain this relationship has brought, and the **future conditional tense** suggests that the negative emotions will not diminish with time. The regular **structure** could reflect how the poet is attempting to control his enormous grief by rigid, unchanging stanzas. Both poets warn us that when love fails, it brings great pain; pain that endures for a long time.

Essential Exam Tips

- ☑ Leave time for checking through your work. One tip is to check each paragraph as you finish it before starting the next one.
- ☑ Use formal language throughout your response. Not all exam boards will be assessing your spelling, punctuation and grammar on this question but you should still write as well as you can.

Desire: Question & Answer

How do the poets present ideas of desire in 'Porphyria's Lover' and 'Love's Philosophy'?

☑ Both poems explore desire as a powerful emotion

Desire is presented as an incredibly powerful emotion that consumes the speakers in both poems. Shelley explores how romantic love brings great pleasure as he refers to light sources found in nature: **'and the sunlight' 'and the moonbeams'**. He uses *images* of light to symbolise hope and joy, emulating the optimism and rapture experienced by the love between two humans. The *anaphora* reinforces the strength and power of these emotions as it builds up a vivid *image* of bright light that dazzles and gives great positive energy. It is significant that he mentions light by day and by night, suggesting that love and desire are perpetual (constant) emotions. This power of desire is also presented as compelling in 'Porphyria's Lover', yet here the overwhelming desire is chilling rather than celebratory and joyous. The narrator desires Porphyria in such an intense way that he needs to exclude everyone else. When she comes to his cottage, the speaker says **'That moment she was mine, mine'**. The *repetition* here of the *possessive pronoun* **'mine'** shows the narrator's need to own her and to control her. The sense of drama here increases as the narrator begins to show us his psychopathic tendencies and his inability to control his strong desire to possess her.

☑ Both poets use nature to explore ideas of desire

Both poets use nature to explore ideas of desire. Shelley was a Romantic poet and embraced the beauty and power of nature. Having lived in mountainous Switzerland, he was inspired by the scenery; in the line **'see the mountains kiss high Heaven'**, there is positive *imagery* with the *personification* of a mountain reaching up to caress the sky, celebrating the soaring strength of nature and also, perhaps, showing sexual connotations with the physical contact between sky and mountain. Nature is also used to show ideas about the power of love and desire in 'Porphyria's Lover', but the *tone* is very different as desire is shown to bring great pain. The opening of the poem is dense with *pathetic fallacy* as the wind **'tore the elm-tops down for spite'**. Browning is establishing a bleak, ominous atmosphere through the *personification* of the wind which is seen as vicious in the *verb* **'tore'** and malicious with the *noun* **'spite'**. The destructive weather reflects the narrator's mood; the *metaphor* of the speaker with his **'heart fit to break'** reveals that the persona's emotions are being pulled apart, just as the wind is pulling apart the landscape. The opening is effective, creating a sense of unease and uncertainty with the volatile weather and the promise of violent emotional pain. The Gothic genre was popular with Victorian writers and its conventions are clearly used in this poem by Browning; he presents us with a wild, almost supernatural landscape where rational human logic is being overwhelmed by natural and supernatural influences. The power and also the pain of desire is clearly evident to the reader through this presentation of nature as wild and destructive.

☑ Both poets structure their poems to show ideas about desire

Shelley structures his poem as two octaves that build up a clever argument, adding layers of logic and persuasive devices to convince his lady that she must give in to her desire and be his lover. Each stanza ends with a *rhetorical question* that engages the listener and ensures that the argument is seen as convincing. Interestingly, it is *structurally* so cleverly put together that it rings of a cynical attempt at seduction rather than as a genuine outpouring of love. The sense of artifice or falsehood is even more noticeable if we remember that Shelley uses religion, referencing **'High Heaven'** with **'divine'** to create a *semantic field* of religious *imagery* to strengthen his point. The implication here is that the pairing of man and woman is a natural act that is blessed by God and so here Shelley is using religion to strengthen his argument. This would be especially relevant to most 19th century readers to whom Christianity was a fundamental part of life. Yet Shelley himself was an atheist and so we wonder whether his use of religion is a manipulation to convince the object of his desire, following in the footsteps of other poets such as Marlowe who wrote persuasively in order to seduce. Browning also *structures* his poem to explore ideas about desire and chooses the form of a *dramatic monologue* to allow us insight into the mind of a murderer. A completely regular *rhyme scheme* runs through the poem, suggesting a persona who is absolutely in control. Despite the brutal murder, the *rhyme scheme* never alters which suggests a calm, callous lack of feeling on the part of the narrator. Alternatively, the regular, rigid *rhyme scheme* could suggest that his mind is so deranged that, to him, the murder is simply a normal, regular event.

☑ Both poets show how ideas of desire and control are linked

The form and *structure* of both poems reflect the control the men have in achieving their desire, yet, interestingly, Shelley and Browning explore how desire also leads to a loss of control. Shelley ends his poem with a *rhetorical question* which is intentionally disarming as he asks **'What is all this sweet work worth/ If thou kiss not me?'** Shelley is using it to carefully manipulate his potential lover because it almost forces the questioned lady to answer 'Of course I will kiss you!' To reject him would be to reject nature and God and the laws of the universe. This last line of the poem works as a neat ending to the culmination (conclusion) of ideas that have been built up throughout the poem and encourages the lady he is addressing to throw caution and social rules to the wind and embrace him, giving in to her physical desire. The narrator in 'Porphyria's Lover' also loses control as he is unable to bear the thought of losing his lover so wraps her hair **'three times her little throat around'**. Interestingly, although the narrator appears to have lost control, the precise detail of **'three times'** does show a calm, calculating murderer who is making deliberate choices. The *adjective* **'little'** reflects Porphyria's vulnerability, directing the reader's response of horror and pity for her while the *enjambment* horribly captures the movement of the hair being wrapped around her neck. The simple *statement* - **'And strangled her'** - which comes at the start of the line, jolts and shocks the reader. There is no tone of the confessional here, no tone of guilt; the narrator is simply stating facts, much as he might say 'and walked home'. Desire is so powerful that he has broken society's rules and committed murder, while in 'Love's Philosophy' desire also overrides rules of acceptable behaviour yet in a joyous and fulfilling way.

Essential Exam Tips

- ☑ **Spend five minutes planning your answer; this helps you organise your ideas into a structure that is clear for the examiner.**
- ☑ **Aim for about four detailed paragraphs; your response will be evaluated on quality not quantity but it's difficult to make your response good if it's brief or lacking in detail.**

Conflict: Question & Answer

Compare how conflict within relationships is presented in 'Neutral Tones' and 'Winter Swans'.

☑ Start with the point that conflict in relationships is painful

'Neutral Tones and 'Winter Swans' explore conflict within relationships, and the pain that this brings. However, while Hardy's poem is unremittingly bleak in that the conflict is irreparable and final, Sheers' poem offers us hope that conflict in a relationship can be resolved. Yet both poets acknowledge that the conflict in relationships is painful. In 'Winter Swans', Owens uses **pathetic fallacy** of the stormy setting and the **image** of a suffocating earth to establish an uneasy atmosphere. The speaker notes that the **'waterlogged earth (is) gulping for breath'**. The **personification** of the muddy ground struggling to breath is an uncomfortable **image**; the natural world is unsettled and so reflects the couple's disharmonious relationship. Perhaps the couple is also struggling to speak and to communicate. The poem comes from Sheers' anthology entitled Skirrid Hill where many poems deal with isolation and separation. Similarly, Hardy uses nature to reflect a troubled relationship by showing us a cold, barren landscape that is **'ash'** and **'grey'**. The dull colours reflect the speaker's relationship, which has been washed of life or emotion. The **'ash'** tree has hints of a fire that has burnt out, leaving nothing but dust. It **symbolises** the burning out of passion as love is traditionally linked to heat but here the fire, and the relationship, is burnt out and is dead. This is also reflected in the description of the sky with its white **'God-curst sun'**, creating an incredibly negative atmosphere through the sun's unnatural colour. We wonder whether the couple are being punished by God in the failure of their relationship; Hardy's writings consistently explore this sense of punishment, of an unfeeling, cold divine presence which treats humans harshly.

☑ Move to the point that both poets show conflict is hard to resolve

The conflict in both poems is hard to resolve. In Sheers' poem, the couple **'skirted the lake, silent and apart'**. The hard **consonance** of the 'k' and 't' sounds echo the rift between the couple; the sounds are not soft and moulded together but jarring and sharp. The **verb 'skirted'** refers to the couple walking around the lake but it also suggests there has been a row, an issue to be skirted or avoided, and this sense of a stalemate is reinforced with the two **adjectives 'silent and apart'** which are positioned at the end of the line to emphasise the isolation that the conflict has brought. The water in the lake is still and stagnant, **symbolic** of the way that the couple cannot move on until the conflict has been resolved. Still water is also used in 'Neutral Tones' as the couple stand by a pond. Here, the conflict is so damaging that it has killed their relationship and cannot be resurrected or resolved. The speaker describes his lover's smile **'like an ominous bird a-wing…'** The **simile** compares the lover's grin to a prophetic bird of doom, as an omen that forecasts the end of their relationship. The **ellipsis** marks a turning point in the poem, as the poet finishes his memory and it also suggests that the memory lingers on in the poet's mind. It could well be a real memory as Hardy's first marriage was an unhappy one and his difficult relationships with women are reflected here in this poem.

☑ Make the point that the poems differ in the resolution of conflict

Sheers shows us how conflict can be resolved through the swans who **'mate for life'** and who spark a sense of resolution between the couple as their hands join together **'like a pair of wings settling after flight'**. The **simile** shows how the couple are now like the faithful swans, joining together to stand by each other despite rocky times. The word **'pair'** places them together, sealing the sense of unity while **'settling'** implies the conflict has been resolved and brings a **tone** of peace and resolution. All relationships experience conflict at some point and Sheers explores this universal experience, perhaps giving a message of hope that it is possible to work through difficult times. However, Hardy presents a different message: that conflict is devastating and cannot resolved as his pain lingers on. Hardy's language choices clearly show bitterness with the statement that **'love deceives'**, revealing his disillusionment with love and suggesting that he is angry and blames his partner for the break-up. Alternatively, it is possible that Hardy is not so much angry as defeated by the conflict. His use of commas in the final stanza creates a disjointed, awkward pace which reflects the speaker's disconnection with the situation. The *repetition* at end **'and' 'and'** with *monosyllabic* words creates a heavy, disillusioned *tone* at the end. Hardy ends his poem on this dull, lifeless *rhythm* to show his lack of emotion about the relationship where conflict has not been resolved but is perhaps accepted as part of life. Certainly, there is a pessimism here that contrasts sharply with Sheers' tentative optimism.

☑ Both poets structure their poems to explore ideas of conflict

Hardy uses *structure* to reflect these pessimistic ideas and emotions associated with the end of a relationship; he uses *tenses* to show us how it is very difficult to put a failed relationship behind us. In 'Neutral Tones', the last *stanza* is in the *present tense*, suggesting that the memory is fresh in his mind and that he revisits it. This is also encapsulated (shown) by the *circular structure*; the poem begins and ends with the pond, reflecting how the event has influenced his life. Like the still water of the pond does not move, he also has not moved on; the *circular structure* shows that he cannot escape this unhappy memory. However, the *structure* of 'Winter Swans' brings a message of hope. Most of the poem is written in three line *stanzas*, the odd number reflecting a lack of unity, and so the opening *stanzas* show us a fractious relationship. Yet there is a *volta* in the line **'until the swans came'** where the mood of the poem changes. The swans in their natural setting now brings hope to the estranged couple and the poem finishes with a two line *stanza*, *symbolising* the pairing of the two lovers and reflecting how, at the end, the couple have healed their disagreement. The poem gives the reader optimism that conflict and pain in relationships is inevitable but can be resolved while Hardy leaves us in no doubt that relationships are doomed to inflict lasting pain on us.

Essential Exam Tips

☑ **Don't worry about writing a long conclusion. It isn't necessary.**

☑ **If you can, compare how both poets use form and structure.**

Marriage: Question & Answer

Compare how marriage is presented in 'Singh Song!' and 'The Farmer's Bride'.

☑ **Start with the point that the marriages presented in the two poems are very different**

In 'Singh Song', the speaker's marriage is presented as a lively, positive relationship as he enjoys the physical aspect to marriage, describing how they **'made luv/ like vee rowing through Putney'**. The light, tripping *rhythm* and *internal rhyme* of **'vee' 'Putney'** adds to the sense of the poem being a song, perhaps a love song to his unconventional bride. It gives the poem a jaunty tone, showing the speaker's delight in his wife while the humorous *simile* which shows teamwork and physical harmony tells us that they take great pleasure in their sex life. This contradicts the stereotype of the loveless arranged marriage sometimes associated with Indian marriages. However, the marriage in 'The Farmer's Bride' is a relationship where there is no such physical closeness. The end *stanza* highlights the isolation between the farmer and his wife as he says that his wife **'sleeps up in the attic there / Alone, poor maid'**. The *enjambment* emphasises their physical separation, and their loneliness is emphasised with the *caesura* after **'alone'**. We sympathise with the farmer here; he is respecting her desire to not share his marriage bed and the *epithet* **'poor maid'** reveals his feelings of kindness and bewilderment to his unusual wife. We feel pity for her as well as she is so terrified of the marriage bed and so isolated. The companionship of the couple in 'Singh Song', who enthusiastically work together at the sexual side to their relationship, is completely absent in the farmer's marriage.

☑ **Move to the point that the marriages are presented in very different settings**

The couple in 'Singh Song!' live out their marriage in a town or city and Nagra uses details such as **'concrete-cool'** to show the rather grim urban environment. The hard sounds of the 'c' show the dull, functional environment of the city or town and this contrasts with the soft *alliteration* of the **'silver stool'** where the speaker finds romance and companionship with his wife. It is significant that, despite the mundane, dreary surroundings, the couple can still find romance and magic, encapsulated by the positive *adjective* **'silver'**. Interestingly, the setting for the marriage in 'The Farmer's Bride is the opposite, as the couple live in a rural community surrounded by nature, yet this does not impact positively on their marriage. The farmer uses natural *imagery* to describe his wife who is **'sweet as the first wild violets, she, To her wild self'**. The beautiful *simile* suggests the farmer's admiration for his wife as he uses the image of a flower as a reference from his daily life that he is familiar with. Yet while this *simile* links the wife to nature, it also links her to the wild and not to 'normal' society. The wife is seen as outside conventional society, challenging the norms of Victorian womanhood as she does not give herself meekly to her husband. The *repetition* of **'wild'** is used by the poet to emphasise the farmer's confusion as to how to form a relationship with someone so unconventional, so untamed. Mew was herself unconventional, wearing trousers and keeping her hair short; it could well be that she is using her poem to show another woman who struggled to conform to 'normal' society.

☑ **Make the point that both marriages show how the couples face challenges**

Both poets show us how marriages face problems and conflicts. The Indian couple face strains in their relationship; this is clear in the anger shown as the bride is **'effing at my mum'**. The swearing indicates her frustration and rebellion which could come from the external factors that the couple are having to deal with: racism, parental pressure, hard work. The poem's *structure* reflects this pressure as the italicised *stanzas* starting with **'Hey Singh, ver yoo bin?'** work as a *chorus* which captures the racist attitudes of some people towards immigrants. The *repetition* of the chorus shows us the regularity of the customers' complaints and the relentless casual racism that the couple have to contend with. This marriage is not one of complete bliss, and the same is true of the marriage in 'The Farmer's Bride' where the wife is locked up after trying to escape and **'we...turned the key upon her, fast'**. The finality of her capture is emphasised by the poet's use of the comma which creates a pause that underlines the security of the next word- **'fast'**. This creates a sense of imprisonment as she is locked up like an animal, her freedom as a human being to move around completely curtailed. In the 19th century society, women were legally placed under the control of their husbands and the farmer has the right to lock her up; indeed, the use of the *pronoun* **'we'** suggests that he had local support from villagers who would have seen it as his right to bring his difficult wife home. However, Mew was writing at the time of the emerging Suffragette movement, so Victorian readers might well have started to question this attitude of oppression and control. Interestingly, locks and keys are referred to in 'Singh Song' as well; the speaker is defying his father's wishes of wanting him to keep the shop open and work all hours of the day and **'ven nobody in, I do di lock'**. He would rather be making love with his new bride, showing the clash of generations and attitudes. There is a hint at a repressive culture in **'the lock'** and he is treated as a naughty child when he sneaks upstairs. Yet it is he who chooses to turn that lock, to enjoy his wife's company; he is taking control of his daily life. And, unlike the speaker in 'The Farmer's Bride' who uses a lock and key to control his relationship, in 'Singh Song!' there is a sense that the wife is happy with this and that they are complicit in a desire for privacy.

☑ Finish with the point that the poems end by presenting opposite portraits of marriage

The relationship between the speaker and his wife is a strong one and the ending of the poem shows the couple sitting together looking at the moon: **'From di stool each night I say/-Is priceless baby'**. The *repetition* of these lines **'from di stool'** show that it's a nightly ritual between them, emphasising their closeness and joy in each other. He clearly values his wife as '**priceless**', above money, perhaps showing a shift in attitude from his parents' and grandparents' attitudes to marriage. In contrast, the ending to 'The Farmer's Bride' shows division in the relationship as the farmer longs for his estranged wife, thinking of **'the brown of her – her eyes, her hair, her hair!'** Unlike the positive ending to **'Singh Song'** with its romantic harmony, **'The Farmer's Wife'** ends on a painful ending to the poem. The farmer's lust is evident in the focus of her physical characteristics and the *repetition* here emphasises how his frustrated desire is at the forefront of his mind while the *fragmented* line with the *dash* shows the breaking down of his narrative as his emotions overwhelm him. It is interesting that he mentions '**eyes**' and '**hair**' but nothing to do with her mouth or lips. This emphasises her silence in this marriage and the lack of communication and, indeed, the form of the poem, a *dramatic monologue*, ensures that the wife is not given a voice. This is the same form as 'Singh Song', and both poets show us ideas of marriage from the male perspective, yet the marriages presented are polar opposites in terms of the happiness or unhappiness that they bring.

Essential Exam Tips

- ☑ Try to include your own ideas and interpretations of the poems.
- ☑ Keep an eye on the time. Write the time that you need to have finished this poetry question on a piece of paper and stick to it. If you run over too much, your response to the next question will suffer.

Separation: Question & Answer

Compare how poets present ideas about being apart in 'Sonnet 29- I think of thee!' and one other poem in 'Love and Relationships'.

☑ Start with the point that the speakers in both poems are living apart

The speakers in both 'Sonnet 29' and 'Letters from Yorkshire' are physically apart from someone that they love or are emotionally close to. In Sonnet 29, the speaker holds her absent lover in her mind constantly. The positive exclamation of **'I think of thee!'** opens the *sonnet* on a declaration of excitement. The **exclamation mark** suggests a spontaneous calling out, showing the persona's happiness as her lover fills her mind. The **pronoun** '**thee**' tells us that she is directly addressing one person and indeed Barrett Browning wrote this *sonnet* and others in the Sonnets of the Portuguese to her fiance, Robert Browning, as an expression of her love. Similarly, the people in 'Letters from Yorkshire' hold each other in their thoughts despite the hundreds of miles between London and Yorkshire. The ease of communication in 21st century England is captured in the line **'our souls tap out messages'**. '**Tap**' is a light, quick *verb* that shows how easy it is for emails to transcend **'icy miles'**; not even bleak weather cannot stop their communication. The **noun 'souls'** is deliberately used to show the intensely personal connection between them. They are communicating at a deep emotional level, similar to the strong emotions that Barrett Browning experiences.

☑ Move to the point that the poets use natural imagery to explore emotions

Both poets use natural *imagery* to explore the emotions that are triggered when people are parted. In his absence, the speaker in Sonnet 29 uses an **extended metaphor** of the speaker's thoughts being **'wild vines'** and her loved one a **'tree'**: these vines **'twine and bud/About thee'**. The natural *imagery* is used to reflect their love and interdependency as the vines **'twine'** or interlace together around the lover. The **enjambment** here echoes the movement of the vine wrapping itself around the tree, showing how their love interconnects together even when they are apart. It is possible that the *imagery* of the vines comes from the Bible, reflecting the sanctity of the emotions that she is feeling. Alternatively, the *image* has sexual connotations with the **'bud'** being a *symbol* for female genitalia and **'twine'** suggesting the physical sexual union of two bodies. Perhaps the *image* covers all of these interpretations; Barrett Browning was highly religious and yet sexual love within the bounds of marriage is something that the Bible celebrates. This *image* of the vines shows how, in his absence, she sustains herself with excited anticipation about their coming union and sees it as something natural, holy and sexually fulfilling. Similarly, the poet in 'Letters from Yorkshire' uses natural *imagery* to express the connection in the relationship but not in a sexual way. Instead, the poet uses a nature *metaphor* to show the connection between the two correspondents as the man in Yorkshire writes a letter **'pouring air and light into an envelope'**. This beautiful *metaphor* captures the positivity of this letter correspondence, suggesting the hope and brightness that the letter will bring the reader and the pleasure the writer has in scribing his letter. The *verb* '**pouring**' suggests a fluidity, a smoothness of communication, that again creates a pleasant *image*. This use of a nature *metaphor* connects the woman with the landscape that she is missing out on.

☑ Move to the point that the absence can be difficult in different ways

Separation can be seen to cause difficulties in relationships. Arguably, the persona in 'Sonnet 29' becomes obsessive about her absent lover, her thoughts being like vines that cover the tree so fully that **'there's nought to see'**. The absence seems to foster a possessive love as the *image* suggests that she is smothering him with love and showing an all-consuming need to contain her beloved, to completely immerse herself in his life. It does seem potentially unhealthy. In the same way, the separation of the speaker in 'Letters from Yorkshire' creates an unhealthy vacuum. The speaker is in urban London, far from her native rural Yorkshire and this seems to cause a disconnect or emptiness. She asks

'Is your life more real because you dig and sow?' and this question perhaps shows the doubt that the speaker has over her life choices. The poem is autobiographical and Dooley did move away from her roots, yet this experience of moving away from where one is born is a very common one, leaving many people with a feeling of regret or discontent. However, there is, perhaps, an acceptance in the poem that both ways of life are valid. The speaker references her work as she produces a '**heartful of headlines**'. Even though she is not living with nature in Yorkshire, her way of life is important as she helps process news stories that help the world communicate.

☑ **Finish by examining how *structure* is used by the poets to show ideas of separation**

Despite the distance between the speaker and Yorkshire, the poet shows us how it is possible to allay the pain of separation through communication. The lack of strict rhythm or rhyme reflects the ease and naturalness of this communication; the letter, the email and the headline show the importance of communication between people, from private individuals to a much wider public. This communication is also shown through the *enjambment* that connects most of the *stanzas*, for example, **'seeing the seasons/ turning'**. The *sibilance* of **'seeing' 'seasons'** also helps create a soft gentle *rhythm* to the phrase, mirroring the smooth, cyclical changing of the seasons and reflecting how time gently, inexorably moves on and how change- including a change in one's location- is natural. This *free verse* of a 20th century poem is very different from the controlled *sonnet* form that Barrett Browning, writing in the 19th century, uses. *Sonnets* are a traditional form for love poems, and this is a very personal, very passionate love poem. A *sonnet* also presents an argument and this *sonnet* declares how the lover consumes her thoughts when apart and when he is actually with her, he completes her. This conclusion works to show how the lovers will eventually be together and make each other joyfully complete and, while in 'Letters from Yorkshire' the speaker does not return to Yorkshire, the communication keeps her connection alive. In both poems, the speakers do not agonise over their separation but deal with it in differing degrees of acceptance.

Essential Exam Tips

☑ **Try to embed quotations within sentences.**

☑ **Don't write out the full titles of the longer poems. 'Sonnet 29' is fine as a shortened version of 'Sonnet 29- I think if thee!'**

Parent and Child: Question & Answer

Compare the ways poets present relationships between a parent and a child in 'Walking Away' and 'Mother, any distance'.

✓ Start with the point that both poets show loving relationships

Armitage explores a young man's relationship with his mother as they measure for furnishings in his new home. The poem affectionately examines the mother-son relationship and how it changes as the son takes a step towards independence. This idea of a child becoming more independent is also explored in 'Walking Away' although this poem is written from a parent's point of view. Both poems present loving relationships and this is evident even in the title of Armitage's poem: 'Mother, any distance'. The title suggests that the son will always need his mother and be connected to her. Indeed, at no point in the poem is the connection between the two severed; they both hold onto the tape measure no matter how high he climbs away from her, reflecting the continuous bond of parent and child. In Day-Lewis's poem, the **tone** is equally affectionate as the speaker addresses his son as he remembers his son moving away from him at school to play football. 'Walking Away' is used as a title and is also used in the last **stanza**, holding the memory and the poem tightly together. The use of the **present tense** gives the poem a sense of immediacy shows how clear this memory still is, still very fresh in his mind as he remembers the protectiveness he felt for his young son. **Fragmented speech**, shown through the use of **dashes**, shows how the poet is pulling up the details of his memory and these dashes also create pauses which allow us to experience the strong emotions of the experience. It is also an experience that almost any parent can relate to, watching their children move away from them in the playground at school.

✓ Move to the point that the poems both show how relationships between parents and children change

In **'Mother, any distance'**, the young man is exploring his new home where he will live independently of his parent. Modern parents encourage their children to value independence and move out of the family home and the mother in this poem is clearly doing this. The speaker is relishing this new freedom and he describes his movements as a **'space walk'** which is a humorous **image** showing the son bounding free from even that most basic of rules. He is separating from his mother and his life, free from parental control, will be an exciting, unknown adventure. Yet the empty rooms are are compared to vast open areas of land such as **'acres'** and **'prairies'**. These **metaphors** suggest that the speaker feels daunted by the unfamiliar unknown space; he is not yet completely independent. Similarly, in 'Walking Away' the boy is not certain about his movement away from his father and the **verbs 'drifting'** and **'scatter'** show an anxiety about this parting. The boy isn't clear about his path away from his parent and seems vulnerable because of this. The **enjambment** between these two lines reflects the boy's hesitation as he moves away and capture these first, cautious steps of independence.

✓ Make the point that the poems show the pain of changing relationships

The parent in 'Walking Away' is also unsure about letting his son go. It is a time of flux for both of them and the language captures this anxiety. The speaker uses a space **simile** to describe the boy's movement towards independence as **'like a satellite/ Wrenched from its orbit'**, reminding us of how a young child gravitates to his or her parents, moving around the parent, staying close to him or her. Yet here the satellite is **'wrenched from its orbit'**. The **enjambment** highlights the physical and symbolic separation and also emphasises the impact of the **verb 'wrenched'** at the start of the next line. **'Wrenched'** is a painful **verb**, reflecting the distress of the father as he realises his son is moving further away from him. In a similar way, there is emotional conflict in 'Mother, any distance'. The mother holds the tape measure tightly; the **verb 'pinch'** is used to show just how firm her grip is.

'**Pinch**' has connotations with being uncomfortable or in pain; maybe his mother is desperately trying to hold on to her son who is leaving her and this is causing tension. This tension is also reflected in the way that the son and mother use different terminology to measure the space: '**centimetres**' and '**inch**' show the difference in approach created by the age gap. It could also reflect how the son needs his independence; their measurements are inherently different as the same distance will be one figure in centimeters and another in inches. There is a sense of a clash here, an incompatibility between them as the poet shows the change in their relationship with the son choosing his own way of recording and living his life.

☑ Finish with the point that both poets present acceptance of change

The *structure* of 'Mother, any distance' reflects the idea of breaking free, starting with the semblance (appearance) of a formal *sonnet* structure with a *rhyming couplet* '**doors/floors**' and a four line verse. By the end, the final *stanza* is five lines long with an irregular meter, showing the son stepping outside parental limits and choosing his own path. However, the poem finishes with another *rhyming couplet* '**sky/fly**', implying that the mother and son are still connected; despite the relationship inevitably changing, they will still be close. Their continued bond is cemented in the single word sentence '**Anchor**' which emphasises the importance of his mother as the person that holds steady in his life, the person that he can always rely on. She is a constant in his life. Similarly, the speaker in 'Walking Away' accepts the change within the relationship. The final *stanza* acts as a conclusion to the situation as the speaker states '**And love is proved in the letting go**'. The word '**proved**' means that the need for a parent to allow his child to separate from him has been shown to be true. Cecil Day-Lewis had a difficult relationship with his own father and there is a poignancy perhaps that he has such clear love and care of his own son. The son of a clergyman, Day-Lewis also uses religion to help comfort him, referring to God letting Jesus come to earth in the line '**God alone could perfectly show**'. Yet within the acceptance there is a lasting pain as the *verb* '**gnaws**' shows a regret and pain rather than acceptance. There is a sense of persistence, of something nagging away. Both poets allow us to experience the range of emotions experienced by a child growing up and they also reflect the universal experience of all parents.

Essential Exam Tips

- ☑ If you run out of time, jot down the ideas you were planning to move onto as bullet points. The examiner will read these and give you some credit.
- ☑ Keep quotations short and focused; don't copy out big chunks of the printed poem.

Memory: Question & Answer

Compare how relationships are presented through memory in 'Before You Were Mine' and 'Eden Rock'.

☑ Start with the point that both poems use memory to explore relationships

Both 'Before You Were Mine' and 'Eden Rock' explore positive memories of parents. Causley remembers a childhood picnic at a place named 'Eden Rock' which is a reference to the Garden of Eden, a place of perfect paradise. This suggests the idyllic nature of the place in Causley's childhood memory, and certainly the memory is a happy one. Causley's memory of a perfect family picnic is one which many readers can relate to. It shows our tendency to look back at childhood memories with rose coloured spectacles (seeing the memory as perfect) and not remember the negative aspects. The speaker remembers how his parents gestured to him: **'Leisurely,/They beckon to me'**. **'Leisurely'** is a peaceful **adverb**, creating a sense of calm and peace, and this slow, gentle pace is further created through the **enjambment** here, aided by the use of the comma which acts as a **caesura**. This reflects the sense that the poet is savouring (enjoying) his happy memory. Duffy also enjoys the memory of her mother who used to dance with her daughter on the way home from church, referencing the Catholic upbringing. The final **stanza** opens with the quick sounding, **monosyllabic** words **'cha cha cha'** that vividly create a sense of fun and movement. Their position at the start of the **stanza** creates a lively energetic opening to the **stanza**, reinforcing her mother's vitality (liveliness) and the happy times that the mother and daughter used to have together. Although Causley's memory is relaxed and gentle and Duffy's is energetic and lively, both poets show how their memories are pleasurable ones.

☑ Move to the point that these memories bring a mixture of emotions

The predominant emotions in 'Eden Rock' are happiness and love. The natural colour of his mother's hair - **'wheat'**- works well with the setting which sits as backdrop for the natural relationship between parents and child. It is a warm, positive colour, helping to create a sense of a positive memory and a sense of the poet's affection for his parents. Yet the memories bring other emotions other than pleasure. There is a sense of nostalgia in 'Eden Rock' as the poet remembers a place and time that are gone. Just as Adam and Eve were forced to leave Eden, he is unable to return to his childhood and he only has memories of his now dead parents. These memories are strong ones and the very clear **images** of his dead parents reflect his own certainty and belief in his faith: that, as a Christian, he will be re-born and see his parents again. There is a whole array of emotions in Duffy's poem. The conversational **tone** and **direct address** of **'whose small bites on your neck, sweetheart?'** create an intimate feel, as does the endearment (loving word) **'sweetheart'**. The speaker loves her mother and wants to know her history, probing the past as she tries to extend her relationship and connect further with her mother. However, the question also perhaps suggests a regret that the daughter will never know her mother as the young carefree girl and so eagerly questions her to learn her history second hand. Alternatively, the phrase could indicate jealousy as the persona's need for her mother to share everything, even her past, shows a real possessiveness. Perhaps it reveals a mixture of all these feelings, reflecting the multi-layers of the mother-daughter relationship.

☑ Both poets present the memories as vivid ones

The details in the memory help reflect the relationships and emotions. The parents' voices help create a vivid scene in 'Eden Rock' as they call to him that **'crossing is not as hard as you might think'.** Their words are encouraging and supportive, reflecting the role of a parent which is to help and to motivate. We see how the speaker's parents are there for him all through his life, right to the end. Their love and support is life-long. Causley's father died when he was still a child so his view of him, encouraging and supportive could well have been the idealised view of a child's perception of a parent. Duffy also captures a vibrant memory as she says **'Your polka-dot dress blows round your legs. Marilyn.'** The speaker describes her mother as a young woman whose dress is blowing round her legs, like the famous photo of Marilyn Monroe, a 50s film star. The *image* is one of freedom and flirtatiousness, showing how the mother's life was once very different. It is possible that the speaker is looking at an old photograph of her mother, or even remembering looking as a child at the photograph. However, the use of the *present tense* suggests that this is an event happening now. This shows the power of memories, both real and imagined. We do question the accuracy of the memories, though, as the speaker was never there with her mother; she is imagining her mother rather than remembering her. Lines between real memory and the imagination are blurred in 'Eden Rock' as well as **'the sky lightens as if lit by three suns'**. In a prosaic (commonplace) poem full of everyday details, this is a moment which seems extraordinary as the sky changes colour. The light dominates the sky, drains it of colour and **'whitens'** it. There is a suggestion of an otherworldliness as the bright light suggests a vision of heaven. The *simile* **'as if lit by three suns'** links the three people: the mother, father and child. This highlights their togetherness and is also perhaps a suggestion that the time has come for the speaker to join his parents in death. The brightness creates a positive *image* of death and what comes afterwards. The **'three suns'** is also suggestive of the Holy Trinity (Father, Son, Holy Spirit) and reflects Causley's religious beliefs. Perhaps the memory is more an allegory of approaching death and the afterlife.

☑ Both poets structure their poems to reveal the memories

Both poets structure their poems to reveal their memories. In 'Eden Rock', the first five *stanzas* detail the memory but there is a change from the regular *structure* of the poem at the end with the last *stanza*: **'I had not thought it would be like this'**. The final line is separated, as the speaker moves from describing a memory to communicating his own thoughts. The separation reflects the separation of memory from real life, and it also perhaps shows the division of life from death. This final line is very simple. The *monosyllabic* words create a rather childish note of wonder and so creates a beautiful end to the poem. There is a sense of pleasure in that he will see his dead parents again as they were in his memory as a young couple, that the move to death will be a natural, pleasant move. This natural move is illustrated in the movement of the line away from the rest of the poem. However, in 'Before You Were Mine', the persona moves constantly between memories, both real and imagined. The use of the *present tense* gives the memories an immediacy and vivacity (liveliness) that is compelling, and also helps weave the strong relationship between the mother and daughter firmly together. This connection is also cemented through the *repetition* of the phrase **'Before you were mine'** which connects the *stanzas*. The poem ends with this phrase, showing the finality of the end of the mother's young, carefree life. By the end of the poem, she is rooted in her role as mother. In both poems, the poets allow us to see the vibrancy and warmth of their memories, exploring how memories are an integral part of our relationships with others.

Essential Exam Tips

- ☑ Most of the exam boards require you to write about context. If you need to write about context, try to weave it into your answer.
- ☑ Use the poet's surname! It sounds silly but you do have to think about how the ideas are being presented and what the poet is doing. So try 'Shelley presents' or 'Browning creates' or 'Duffy uses'.

Older people: Question & Answer

Compare how relationships with older people are presented in 'Follower' and one poem of your choice.

☑ Start with the point that the speakers in both poems value the older person

In **'Climbing My Grandfather'** and **'Follower'**, the speakers value the older person that they describe. Heaney writes a moving tribute to his farmer father, showing a respect for the man and his work in the *simile* **'his shoulders globed like a full sail strung'** which uses nautical terminology to describe his father as physically impressive and strong. The *image* suggests stateliness and also a sense of grace as there is a smoothness to the phrase captured in the assonance which reflects his natural ability at the ploughing. The *image* also gives us a sense of the size of his father to the small child, looking up at his impressive father; the narrator is awed by the impressive size of his father who is as large as a 'full sail' and there is a *tone* of admiration and respect here. Similarly, Waterhouse values the older person that he describes: his grandfather. Waterhouse uses the *extended metaphor* of mountaineering to describe the speaker's memories of clambering over his grandfather as a child. The poem is written as one *stanza* without a break, showing the continuous action of the boy climbing up the bulk of his grandfather. The *prepositions* **'First… on… at… then'** show the progression of the child as he crawls over the old man and are also a *structural* device to move the reader through the process of getting to see the grandfather's body and to see glimpses of his personality. As the child ascends, Waterhouse presents a range of positive *images*: a **'firm shoulder… smiling mouth'**. There is a sense of reliability in the *adjective* **'firm'** and kind good humour in the **'smiling mouth'**, showing a sense of respect for this man and also using a *tone* of admiration. The details also show a closeness between the old man and the young boy as the man allows his grandchild such intimate access and scrutiny of his body at close quarters. Both Heaney and Waterhouse's poems are autobiographical and so reflect the poets' real life relationships with the older men.

☑ Continue to explore how the poets respect the older person

In 'Climbing My Grandfather', Waterhouse uses precise details to give us clues about the man's personality and lifestyle, telling us that his grandfather had an **'earth-stained hand'**. Here, we have an impression of a man who worked outside, perhaps as a manual labourer or a farmer and so someone who worked hard. It is a reminder to our society, which can treat old people with callousness, that the ageing generation should be valued for their service and experience. It is possible that the **'earth-stained hand'** indicates the grandfather's hobby of gardening and so was someone who was attuned to nature. Waterhouse was passionate about the environment and so it is significant that he notices this detail about his grandfather. There is a clear link between Waterhouse's grandfather and Heaney's father as Heaney describes his father as an outdoors man, ploughing the fields, using both *rhyme* **'sod/plod'** and *half rhyme* **'wake/back'** to reflect the natural pace of his father working. The *half-rhyme* gives the movement of the father ploughing a natural feel as it is not uniform and would be slightly irregular. Heaney grew up in rural Ireland and would have been very familiar with the sight of men ploughing fields. The *half rhyme* also perhaps reflects the relationship between father and son; the son wants to be like his father but cannot be. Although he tries to emulate his father, he doesn't perfectly match. In both poems, we see great respect for the older person.

☑ Move to the point that both poets write from the perspective of a younger person

Waterhouse's title **'Climbing my Grandfather'** is humorous and engaging, establishing the *metaphor* of his grandfather being a mountain. The size of the man shows the young child's view of him as a mountain of a man. The mountain *metaphor* could also symbolise the importance the grandfather had in his grandson's life. Mountains are fixed and significant and this echoes the role of the grandfather in the family and reminds the reader how important the older people in our own families are. They are constants in our lives as we grow up, unlike nursery teachers or playground friends, and often have great influence on us. In the poem, the speaker clambers over his patient grandfather; the **verbs** used **'trying' pull'** suggest that this is a hard climb. This would actually be the case for a small boy climbing up a large adult, but the **verbs** could also suggest that the speaker is trying to remember a dead relative and finding the process of dredging through his memories a difficult one, perhaps because it's so long ago and the memories have faded. Alternatively, the physical **verbs** that reflect real effort could suggest that getting to know someone and to form significant relationships is hard work. In a similar way, 'Follower' is from the perspective of a son who is remembering his father. The speaker knows that, as a child, **'I was a nuisance, tripping, falling/Yapping always'**. There is a clear **statement** here that the boy knew he was in his father's way, a hindrance and not a help to his father's work. The **asyndetic list** here crowds the **verbs** together, emphasising how much of a pain he was being to his father.

☑ Finish with exploring how the relationships are not all positive

This hero worship of Heaney to his father does not last. In the last **stanza** there is a **volta** with the **connective 'But'** that marks a change in perspective. There is also a time shift from a memory of his father to the present day as the speaker states that now **'It is my father who keeps stumbling/Behind me, and will not go away.'** The shift in **tenses** show that the time has changed and with it, so has the relationship as the earlier **tone** of admiration has changed to a **tone** of irritation. His father has become the clumsy, incompetent one causing a nuisance to the son and the **enjambment** emphasises both the clumsiness of the father and the impatience of the son. Heaney shows how there is a natural and painful shift from the hero worship children show their parents to the realisation that parents are just human and therefore frail. There is pain in 'Climbing My Grandfather' as well. The boy is **'Not looking down/for climbing has its dangers'**, possibly reflecting how the drop down seems enormous to the small boy. Yet it could also suggest the dangers of trying to bring back memories; to remember his grandfather is to remember the grief of his death and this is dangerous and hurtful. Perhaps the poet is suggesting that getting to know someone is in itself a dangerous exercise: who knows what you will discover and getting close to someone can make you vulnerable if they let you down or die. There is a sense that forming connections and relationships can be treacherous. Although the poets both present the grandfather and the father as men to admire, both poems have undercurrents that remind us of the pain that can be present in all relationships.

Essential Exam Tips

- ☑ **Underline the focus of the question so you don't stray from answering the question. E.g. in the question above, the focus is relationships with older people.**
- ☑ **Relax and try to enjoy the exam! It will be the last time you ever write about these poems!**

Glossary
Explanation of terms

Accentual verse - poetry where the meter is measured by stressed syllables

Adjective - a word that describes a noun **e.g.** 'three times her <u>little</u> throat around' in 'Porphyria's Lover'

Adverb - word that describes a verb **e.g.** '<u>Leisurely,</u>/They beckon me' in 'Eden Rock'

Alliteration - repetition of the same letter in words next to or near each other e.g. '**c**oncrete-**c**ool' in 'Singh Song!'

Anaphora - repetition of the same phrase at the start of consecutive lines **e.g.** 'and' 'and' in 'Neutral Tone'

Assonance - similar vowel sounds **e.g.** the assonance of the 'o' sound. 'His shoulders globed' in 'Follower'

Asyndetic list - a list which leaves out the conjuction 'and' **e.g.** 'I was a nuisance, <u>tripping, falling/ Yapping</u> always' in 'Follower'

Caesura - pause

Chorus - part of a poem that is repeated

Circular structure - when a poem returns to the same point it starts **e.g.** 'Neutral Tones' begins and ends at the pond.

Consonance - recurrance of similar sounding consonants **e.g.** 's<u>k</u>irted the la<u>k</u>e' in 'Winter Swans'

Contrast- use of opposites

Couplet - two line stanza

Dash - punctuation mark that shows a change of thought or creates a dramatic pause

Declarative statement - a sentence that states a fact **e.g.** 'Thy vows are all broken' in 'When We Two Parted'

Dialect- language from a particular region

Direct address- when the persona speaks

Dramatic monologue - poem where an imagined person speaks to a silent listener **e.g.** 'The Farmer's Bride'

Ellipsis - series of dots to show missing or redundant speech

Enjambment - when a sentence runs onto the next line **e.g.** 'three times her little throat around/ And strangled her' in 'Porphyria's Lover'

Epithet - a descriptive phrase for a person **e.g.** 'poor maid'

Exclamatory sentence - sentence that conveys excitement or emotion **e.g.** 'I think of thee!' in 'Sonnet 29'

Extended metaphor - a metaphor which is developed or used more than once **e.g.** the metaphor of the vines and the tree in 'Sonnet 29'

Fragmented speech - speech which is interrupted **e.g.** 'The brown of her – her eyes, her hair, her hair!' in The Farmer's Bride

Free verse - open form of poetry that does not have fixed patterns of rhyme or rhythm

Future conditional tense - tense that describes a possible future event with a condition **e.g.** 'if I should meet thee' in 'When We Two Parted'

Half-rhyme - partial or near rhyme **e.g.** 'wake' 'back' in 'Follower'

Image - powerful words or phrase that paints a picture in our heads **e.g. 'sunlight' and 'moonbeams"** in 'Love's Philosophy'

Imperative verb - verb that gives a command **e.g. 'See the mountains kiss high Heaven' in 'Love's Philosophy**

Internal rhyme - a rhyme involving a word in the middle of a line and another at the end of the line or in the middle of the next **e.g. 'vee' and 'Putney' in 'Singh Song!'**

Metaphor - descibing a person or object as something else **e.g. 'heart fit to break' in 'Porphyria's Lover'**

Minor sentence - a sentence without a main clause **e.g. 'An expert.' in 'Follower'**

Motif - a repeated idea or image e.g. silence is used as a motif in **'When We Two Parted'**

Monosyllabic words - words with one syllable - **e.g. 'knell in mine ear' in 'When We Two Parted'**

Octave - a stanza with 8 lines

Onomatopoeia - a word that creates the sound it describes **e.g. 'clatter' in 'Before You Were Mine'**

Past tense - tense used to describe events that have already happened

Pathetic fallacy - when weather is used to create a mood or atmosphere **e.g. the wind which 'tore the elm-tops down for spite' in Porphyria's Lover'**

Patriarchal - a society where men are dominant/have power

Personal pronoun - word that replaces a proper noun **e.g. 'we' in 'The Farmer's Wife'**

Personification - when non-human objects or elements are given human qualities **e.g. the wind is described as spiteful in 'Porphyria's Lover'**

Possessive pronoun - word that shows something belongs to someone **e.g. 'she was mine, mine' in 'Porphyria's Lover'**

Prepositions - words that connect things to a time or place **e.g. 'First...on...at... then' in 'Climbing My Grandfather'**

Present tense - tense used to describe events that are happening now

Repetition - when a word or phrase is repeated **e.g. 'she was mine, mine' in 'Porphyria's Lover'**

Rhetorical question - a question that does not need to be answered but makes a point **e.g. 'What are all these kissings worth/If thou kiss not me?' in 'Love's Philosophy'**

Rhyme scheme - pattern of rhyming words that ends lines

Semantic field - group of words on the same subject or theme **e.g. semantic field of cold in 'When We Two Parted'**

Sibilance - repetition of 's' sounds **e.g. 'slow-stepping' in 'Winter Swans'**

Simile - describing a person or object as something else using 'like' or 'as' **e.g. 'as a shut bud that holds a bee' in 'Porphyria's Lover'**

Sonnet - type of poem consisting of 14 lines

Stanza - group of lines which form a verse

Statement - sentence that shows a definite declaration **e.g. 'And strangled her' in 'Porphyria's Lover'**

Structure - the order in which a line/poem is put together

Syndetic list - a list where items are separated by the conjunction 'and' **e.g. 'sparkle and waltz and laugh' in 'Before You Were Mine'**

Tone - mood or atmosphere

Verb - an action word e.g 'glided' in 'Porphyria's Lover'

Volta - turning point in a poem

Vowel sound - sound that a vowel makes **e.g. the long vowel sound in 'slow' in 'Climbing My Grandfather**

Notes